Symbolism is a primary characteristic of mind, deployed and displayed in every aspect of thought and culture. In this important and broad-ranging book, Israel Scheffler explores the various ways in which the mind functions symbolically. This involves considering not only the worlds of the sciences and the arts, but also such activities as religious ritual and child's play. The book offers an integrated treatment of ambiguity and metaphor, analyses of play and ritual, and an extended discussion of the relations between scientific symbol systems and reality. What emerges is a picture of the basic symbol-forming character of the mind.

In addition to philosophers of art and science, likely readers of this book will include students of linguistics, semiotics, anthropology, religion, and psychology.

Symbolic worlds

Symbolic worlds

Art, science, language, ritual

ISRAEL SCHEFFLER

Harvard University

CAMBRIDGE
UNIVERSITY PRESS

Published by the Press Syndicate of the University of Cambridge
The Pitt Building, Trumpington Street, Cambridge CB2 1RP
40 West 20th Street, New York, NY 10011-4211, USA
10 Stamford Road, Oakleigh, Melbourne 3166, Australia

First published 1997
Printed in the United States of America

Library of Congress Cataloging-in-Publication Data
Scheffler, Israel.
Symbolic worlds : art, science, language, ritual / Israel
Scheffler.
p. cm.
ISBN 0-521-56425-5 (hardback)
1. Philosophy of mind.   2. Symbolism.   3. Science – Philosophy.
4. Language and languages – Philosophy.   I. Title.
BD418.3.S34   1997
121'.68 – dc20   96-21483
                                                                CIP

A catalog record for this book is available from the British Library.

ISBN 0-521-56425-5 hardback

Contents

Contents

Acknowledgments

Thanks are due to the following publishers for their permission to reprint materials in this book:

Kluwer Academic Publishers, for "Ritual and Reference," *Synthese*, 46 (March, 1981), pp. 421–37; and "The Wonderful Worlds of Goodman," *Synthese*, 45 (1980), pp. 201–9.

Editions du Centre Pompidou, for "Art Science Religion," *Cahiers du Musée National d'Art Moderne*, 41, Automne 1992, pp. 45–53.

Journal of Aesthetics and Art Criticism, for "Reference and Play," in *Journal of Aesthetics and Art Criticism*, Vol. 50, No. 3, Summer 1992, pp. 211–16; and "Pictorial Ambiguity," same journal, Vol. 47, No. 2, Spring 1989, pp. 109–15.

Hackett Publishing Co., Inc., for Science and the World, Chapter 5, pp. 91–124 of *Science and Subjectivity*, Hackett, Second edition, 1982.

Journal of Philosophy, for Catherine Z. Elgin and Israel Scheffler, "Mainsprings of Metaphor," *Journal of Philosophy*, Vol. 84 (1987), pp. 331–5.

Institut de Philosophie, Université Libre de Bruxelles, for "Ritual Change," *Revue Internationale de Philosophie*, Vol. 46, No. 185, 2–3/1993, pp. 151–60.

University of Illinois Press, for "Ten Myths of Metaphor," *Journal of Aesthetic Education*, Vol. 22, No. 1, Spring 1988, pp. 45–50.

Acknowledgments

M.I.T. Press, for "Worldmaking: Why Worry," in Peter McCormick, ed. *Starmaking*, M.I.T. Press, 1996.

Ridgeview Publishing Company, for "Ambiguity: An Inscriptional Approach" in Richard Rudner and Israel Scheffler, eds. *Logic and Art*, Bobbs-Merrill 1972, now Ridgeview Publishing Company.

I am grateful to Catherine Elgin for permission to reprint our joint article "Mainsprings of Metaphor," in *Journal of Philosophy*, Vol. 84 (1987), pp. 331–5.

I wish also to express my gratitude to JoAnne Sorabella for her excellent and indispensable help in the preparation of the manuscript in its various phases.

Section I
Symbol and reference

Chapter 1

Introduction and background

Symbolism is a primary characteristic of mind, displayed in every variety of thought and department of culture. This book explores aspects of symbolic function in language, science, and art as well as ritual, play, and the forming of worldviews. It restates fundamental themes in my earlier work, follows up prior lines of inquiry in the development of such themes, and deals with several new problems arising in the course of further inquiries.

A study of pragmatism long ago convinced me of the representative character of thought – its functioning as mediated throughout by symbols. My book *Four Pragmatists*[1] presented this view of thought as vigorously argued by C. S. Peirce, William James, G. H. Mead, and John Dewey, and my *Of Human Potential* restated such a view as important for education.[2]

Foremost among the capacities presupposed by human action, I wrote

> is that of *symbolic representation,* in virtue of which intentions may be expressed, anticipations formulated, purposes projected and past outcomes recalled. . . . Human beings are symbolic animals, hence both creators and creatures of culture. . . . the symbolic systems constructed by human beings are not simply changes rung upon some universal matrix, itself sprung from the givens of physics. These several systems are

1 Israel Scheffler, *Four Pragmatists* (London: Routledge & Kegan Paul, 1974).
2 Israel Scheffler, *Of Human Potential* (London: Routledge & Kegan Paul, 1985).

each underdetermined by physical fact, and there is no principle that guarantees perfect harmony and coordination among them. . . . By *symbolic systems*, we have in mind clusters of categories or terms which a person typically displays in certain contexts. Aside from *terms*, we include also non-linguistic vehicles of representation, comprehending the graphical or diagrammatic, the pictorial and plastic, the kinetic and the ritual. What symbolic systems share is the function of ostensible reference to features selected for notice, and of consequent sensitization to properties and relations, inclusions, exclusions, hierarchies and contrasts which organize the world of the subject in characteristic ways.[3]

My account of human nature as ever active and symbol forming has drawn heavily upon the work of the great pragmatic philosophers, as noted. In conceiving of symbolism as comprehending a wide range of nonlinguistic as well as linguistic phenomena, it harks back to a period preceding the most recent era in American philosophy, which has been dominated by a linguistic, logical, and scientific focus. It recalls in fact the more generous pragmatic conception of Peirce, architect of the modern science of signs, concerned with the many dimensions of their functioning. It echoes also Ernst Cassirer's broad definition of man as a symbolic rather than rational animal whose work is exhibited in the several forms of thought comprising human culture.[4] And it reflects the influence of Nelson Goodman's pioneering *Languages of Art,* concerned to develop a broad view of the reference of symbol systems as extending beyond language and encompassing also the arts.[5] Of especial note in the account presented here is the creative character of symbolism, issuing in those radically plural structures that shape the subject's worlds; hence, the title of the present book.

The symbolic worlds to which I refer here include not only the

---

3 Ibid., pp. 17–18.
4 Ernst Cassirer, *An Essay on Man* (New Haven, Conn.: Yale University Press, 1944).
5 Nelson Goodman, *Languages of Art* (Indianapolis, Ind.: Bobbs-Merrill, 1968; Indianapolis, Ind.: Hackett, 1976).

sciences and the arts, but also religious ritual, not only the sober activity of adults, but also child's play. Such worlds embrace not only literal description, but also metaphorical innovation, and whether linguistic or pictorial, they include the ambiguous as well as the straightforward representation. Thus, the major sections to follow include treatments of ambiguity and metaphor, analyses of play and ritual, as well as an extended discussion of the relations between scientific symbol systems and reality.

My book *Beyond the Letter* deals with ambiguity, vagueness, and metaphor in language.[6] The present work treats certain questions that grew from reflection on problems addressed in that book. The treatment of linguistic ambiguity as developed in *Beyond the Letter*, for example, prompted the question of how to interpret the pictorial variety; hence, the analysis of pictorial ambiguity in Chapter 4. The extension of other features of *Beyond the Letter* to the interpretation of ritual and play followed and helped to stimulate certain reflections on the relations of art, science, and religion, represented in Chapter 9.

Beyond the Letter is not, however, a prerequisite for understanding the present work. Indeed, I have tried to compose these chapters so that they stand on their own, calling, where necessary, however, on certain materials reprinted from previous books of mine. Aside from such instances, each chapter to follow has either appeared as an article in a journal or volume of proceedings, or is newly written. Detailed information on sources is given in initial footnotes to the chapters to follow.

I have said that my treatment of symbolism harks back to an earlier period than the most recent one in American philosophy, dominated as the latter has been by a focus on language, logic, and science. It should not be thought, however, that I am in any way opposing logic, science, or linguistic clarity for theoretical purposes. I reject only the restrictions of philosophy to logic, science, or language as objects of study. My interest is after all to further the theory of symbolism. Such theory needs to obey strict methodological canons even as it studies all sorts of symbolic phenomena falling outside the purview of logical discourse. A

6 Israel Scheffler, *Beyond the Letter* (London: Routledge, 1979).

theory must yield understanding, explanation, or insight; unless it obeys special controls, it cannot do so. This explains why my treatment operates theoretically with a very sparse logical and semantic apparatus, while addressing such phenomena as linguistic ambiguity – unwelcome as a feature of theoretical language – and symbolic functions of arts or rites, which fall outside the sphere of theoretical language altogether.

Like my *Anatomy of Inquiry*[7] and *Beyond the Letter,* my approach here has accordingly been nominalistic throughout, eschewing abstract and intensional entities and taking for granted only individual referring entities and individual entities referred to. In the case of language, in particular, such an approach is inscriptionalistic, assuming only the individual tokens (utterances and inscriptions) of the language and the individual things to which such tokens may refer. Such exclusions are motivated by the philosophical criticisms of recent decades. As I wrote in *Beyond the Letter,*

> The significance of such exclusions may be seen by reference to the semantic scheme inherited from the past and widespread in contemporary use.
>
> This scheme recognizes not merely the particular "dog"-utterances and "dog"-inscriptions that historically occur, but also an additional object identified with the word "dog," construed as an abstract entity of some sort – a form, or class, or sequence of sound or letter tokens. It recognizes not merely the individual dogs denoted by the word, but the denotation of the word – an abstract entity identified with the class of dogs denoted. The denotation is, further, construed to be determined by the word's meaning, identified or associated with the attribute of being a dog, itself exemplified by members of the denotation. Concepts, propositions, facts, and states-of-affairs may be introduced additionally, and related in diverse ways to the foregoing objects. The individuation of entities in this scheme, finally, rests at various points on presumed synonymies, analyticities, modal judgments, essences, counterfac-

7 Israel Scheffler, *The Anatomy of Inquiry* (New York: Knopf, 1963).

tual assertions, or intuitive descriptions of the supposed entities in question.[8]

Inscriptionalism, by contrast, takes for granted only the individual things related to one another semantically, and since such things are assumed by any semantic scheme, the theory

> does not add to entities commonly recognized; its interpretations are therefore ontologically acceptable to non-inscriptionalists, although the converse does not hold. Readers who do not share the inscriptionalistic assumptions of the present inquiry may therefore still find interest in its interpretations. They need not take its exclusions in any absolute sense, but only understand them hypothetically, as defining the methodological constraints of the study. They may, however, be assured that notions excluded by these constraints may be reintroduced at will by anyone who does not find them obscure.[9]

I have noted that the work reported here falls within the broad scope of the theory of symbols as conceived by Nelson Goodman. It also owes to Goodman its nominalistic cast as well as its use of particular semantic devices – for example, "exemplification" – developed by him to supplement standard notions of denotation and related ideas. One further and novel semantic thread that runs through a number of the treatments to follow is the notion of mention-selection, introduced for the first time in "Ambiguity in Language," the earliest of the studies included, as Chapter 3, in this volume.

This notion applies to the use of a symbol to refer not only to its instances, but also to its companion symbols. Employed first to enable the analysis of certain aspects of ambiguity, it was next made use of in the analysis of vagueness in *Beyond the Letter*, which briefly noted its relevance also to the interpretation of word magic and to the course of children's learning. In still further applications, the notion proved surprisingly useful in the analysis of pictorial ambiguity (Chapter 4), the interpretation of

---

8 Scheffler, *Beyond the Letter*, p. 9.
9 Ibid.

metaphor (Chapter 7), the understanding of play (Chapter 8), and the analysis of ritual (Chapter 10). It is thus appropriate that the chapter immediately following this one offers a general exposition of mention-selection and an introductory review of the preceding applications, as well as some others.

Section II, on ambiguity, deals with both linguistic and pictorial varieties. Chapter 3 offers an inscriptional analysis of semantically ambiguous terms in the effort to avoid the obscurities and difficulties of the usual accounts. The proposed analysis rests on the notion of *replication*, that is, the sameness of spelling among inscriptions. Thus, for example, two word-tokens may be judged ambiguous if they are replicas of one another but do not denote exactly the same things. On the other hand, the notion of replication is clearly inapplicable to pictures, which are not composed of inscriptions with definitive spelling. The problem of interpreting pictorial ambiguity (e.g., the duck–rabbit, the Necker cube) thus presents itself and is resolved in Chapter 4, with the use of the notion of mention-selection. The treatment lends itself to the interpretation of pictorial metaphor as well.

Section III is concerned with the general problem of metaphor, itself a species of ambiguity in which the literal informs the metaphorical sense of a term. Chapter 5 offers a rebuttal of ten prevalent myths of metaphor. The general point of the chapter is to promote an appreciation of metaphor as a vehicle of serious thought and to understand some of its main features. Chapter 6 comprises a critical discussion of Goodman's contextual view of metaphor and defends a revised contextualism. Chapter 7 responds to criticism of extensional approaches to metaphor and outlines the resources of extensionalism for metaphoric interpretation, among which incidentally, there is the notion of mention-selection.

The role of mention-selection in learning, discussed in Chapter 2, offers a way of interpreting the child's references in play. How is the child's calling his or her broomstick "a horse" to be understood, in view of the fact that the child knows very well that it is not a horse? Responding to E. H. Gombrich's influential discussion of this question, Chapter 8 offers a new approach to the problem of understanding reference in play, using once more the notion of mention-selection. Such understanding also extends to a creative aspect of art – the seeing of one thing as another. Section IV thus incorporates discussions of both play and art, with Chapter 9 addressing relations among the three symbolic enterprises of art, science, and religion. In particular, it asks why science and religion have been thought to be at war, while science and art dwell in peace. If this question is not simply illusory, does the answer to it rest on the allegedly emotive character of art, in contrast with the cognitive nature of both science and religion? Does it perhaps rest on the semantic peculiarities of art in its supposed expressive and exemplificatory functions, which, while cognitive, are to be contrasted with the primarily denotative efforts of science and religion? Or are some other relevant differentia to be found in the pragmatic realm? Chapter 9 explores these possibilities by bringing out certain affinities and contrasts in symbolic function that have not generally been acknowledged and by pointing up the role of authority in both science and religion.

Section V deals with the symbolic character of ritual. Abstracting from the social and historical context of ritual in order to concentrate on its semantic functions, this section emphasizes the cognitive roles of ritual. Following a consideration of the views of Ernst Cassirer and Susanne Langer, Chapter 10 outlines various referential aspects of rites. It discusses notationality of rituals, conditions on the ritual performer, and mimetic rites, in connection with which the notion of mention-selection again plays a role. In the course of its discussion, it develops an important contrast between arts and rites. Finally, it stresses the effect of ritual recurrence and reenactment in the ordering of categories of time, space, action, and community. Chapter 11 takes up the question of ritual change, asking when a change *in* a rite becomes a change *of* a rite. Here the formality of rituals is distinguished from their identity, the alteration of rites is considered along with their birth and death, varieties of ritual specification are taken into account, and the travel of rites across communities is examined.

Finally, Section VI turns to the general question of the relations between world and representation, much debated in recent philosophy. Varieties of realism, antirealism, relativism, and subjectivism have been proposed, defended, and criticized. Chapter 12

9

reviews the debate within the Vienna Circle in the 1930s concerning the presumed connection between science and reality. The debate centered on the status of scientific observation reports, with Otto Neurath insisting that science cannot compare its observations with the world, being wholly enclosed within the domain of propositions, while Moritz Schlick urged that the confirmation statements of science constitute absolutely fixed points of contact between knowledge and reality. Rejecting both these certainty and coherence doctrines, Chapter 12 upholds the view that the import of our scientific statements is inexorably referential, and that such statements are always subject to the twin controls of logic and credibility.

The last three chapters focus on Goodman's conception of worldmaking, introduced in his *Ways of Worldmaking*[10] – a conception according to which the right versions we make, linguistic and nonlinguistic, in turn make the worlds they refer to. Now I agree with Goodman's pluralism and share his general pragmatic temper, upholding the relativity of systems while eschewing subjectivism and nihilism. My pluralist and pragmatic sympathies are evident in my *Four Pragmatists,* and my rejection of subjectivism is clear in my *Science and Subjectivity.*[11]

However, on one point there is fundamental disagreement between Goodman and myself: I have never been able to accept his idea of worldmaking, insofar as he affirms that it is not only versions, but also their objects, that are made by us. Section VI argues, to the contrary, that while we make versions, neither we nor our versions determine them to be right; thus, neither we nor our right versions make their worlds. Chapter 13 presents my general critique of worldmaking. Chapter 14 is a rejoinder to Goodman's reply to this critique. Finally, Chapter 15 responds to Goodman's further defense of his view in his paper "Worldly Worries." In this last chapter, I argue that worldmaking indeed gives us cause to worry and I defend the view that, while we make versions, we do not make them right.

---

10 Nelson Goodman, *Ways of Worldmaking* (Indianapolis, Ind.: Hackett, 1978).
11 Israel Scheffler, *Science and Subjectivity* (Indianapolis: Bobbs-Merrill, 1967; 2nd ed., 1982).

Chapter 2
Denotation and mention-selection

Several years ago, I introduced the semantic notion of mention-selection, which relates a term not to what it denotes but rather to parallel representations of a suitable kind. That is, it relates a term not to what it denotes but rather to those representations that it appropriately captions. Thus, the word "tree" denotes trees, but it mention-selects, that is, serves as a caption for, tree-pictures, tree-depictions, and tree-descriptions; and the word "unicorn" denotes nothing, but it mention-selects, that is, captions, unicorn-pictures, unicorn-descriptions, and unicorn-representations. In this chapter, I offer a general account of the relations between denotation and mention-selection, outlining some of the resources of the latter for interpreting aspects of language learning and some related phenomena of language.

We live in a world of symbols as well as other things, and our commerce with them is itself continually mediated by symbols. As it matures, our thought increasingly grows in its capacity to wield appropriate symbols in reflecting, acting, reasoning, and making. It is not surprising that it takes special effort to disentangle our references to things from our references to the symbols denoting them. Hence, the deliberate practice of employing special notation to mark the distinction in contexts, such as logic,

"Denotation and Mention-Selection" appears here for the first time in its present form; parts of it are drawn from my *Beyond the Letter* (London: Routledge, 1979), Part II (Vagueness), Sections 4, 6, 8.

where theoretical clarity is of utmost importance. Using a term is thus, by the device of quotation, for example, sharply separated from mentioning it.[1] The term "table," unquoted, is used in mentioning certain articles of furniture but is not itself mentioned thereby. On the other hand, the enlarged term consisting of the original framed by quotes mentions the word within its frame, that is, the term tee-ay-bee-el-ee, but neither the compound of that word and its quotation marks, nor any articles of furniture.

Logic is an affair of terms, however, whereas reference may be accomplished by other means as well. A picture of Lincoln, for example, refers to him no less than does the name "Lincoln." Here, however, we confront an apparent deviation from the contrast between use and mention. The very name used to mention President Lincoln is also used to refer to the picture referring to him. For the term mentioning Lincoln also captions a pictorial mention of him. Instead of the picture being mentioned by using a name of it, it is mentioned by using a name of what it itself mentions.

It is true that the term "Lincoln" does not *denote* the picture; the picture is, after all, not the president. But the term appropriately *captions* the picture, that is, selects, applies to, identifies, and, in that sense, mentions the picture. Conscientious use of the device of quotation precludes a term from being used to denote itself, but evidently does not bar its mentioning of a symbol making the identical reference. Nor, once we have distinguished captioning from denotation, is there any reason to restrict it to pictures; a description singling out President Lincoln may be captioned "Lincoln" as well as a picture may. Indeed the very term "Lincoln" may be taken as a caption for "Lincoln"-terms themselves. We have, it is true, here broadened the ordinary use of the notion of a caption to extend it beyond pictures to terms and, indeed, to symbolic representations generally. It is thus useful to introduce the technical term "mention-selection" to cover the broadened interpretation of captioning here proposed.

---

1 See Willard Van Orman Quine, *Mathematical Logic* (Cambridge, Mass.: Harvard University Press, 1947), pp. 23–6.

1 MENTION-SELECTION AND LEARNING

Mention-selection points up certain features of the learning process. The clearest illustration of this fact is provided by terms with null denotation. Such terms cannot be acquired by pointing to the things they apply to. There are no unicorns to point to in teaching a child the use of the word "unicorn." The prevalent myth that learning a term proceeds by ostending the objects of the term breaks down decisively in cases such as these. What may be acquired, indeed, by such ostension is the proper application of the term "non-unicorn," for this term denotes everything. But so does "non-centaur," "non-griffin," and the like. Exhibiting the denotata either of a null term or of its negate will thus fail to make the required meaning differentiations to be acquired by the pupil.

Here we have recourse to other, related representations, to pictures of unicorns and descriptions of unicorns, for example, which can themselves be pointed to and thus differentiated from pictures of centaurs, descriptions of centaurs, and the like. As Goodman has pointed out, the compound terms "unicorn-picture" and "centaur-picture," "unicorn-description" and "centaur-description," are not null even though "unicorn" and "centaur" are null.[2] The child's learning of the latter terms hinges on the appropriate selection and differentiation of related pictures, and other representations, denoted by their respective compounds.

But the child does not typically apply the term "unicorn-picture" in selecting the appropriate objects. He or she uses the original term "unicorn," pointing to the picture and proclaiming "unicorn." Similarly, the child may be required to select appropriate areas of the picture to which to apply the term, indicating thereby that such areas in particular carve out the unicorn-pictures proper and are to be distinguished from the remainders of the pictures in question. Now, in applying the term "unicorn" to a given picture or a particular region of a picture, the child is not exhibiting a denotation of "unicorn"; it is clear to both child and tutor that the picture is itself no unicorn. There are indeed no

2 Nelson Goodman, "On Likeness of Meaning," *Analysis*, 10 (1949), 1–7.

unicorns to be found, and one reason for our confidence in that very fact is that the picture itself shows what an animal would need to look like in order to be a unicorn. The mention-selective use of a term with null denotation aids in the learning of this very denotation itself.

Mention-selective use is, of course, not limited to terms with null denotation, nor is it limited to the learning process. In our typical labeling of a picture of a man "Man" rather than "man-picture," we ourselves apply the term "Man" to select not a man but a picture, our terms acquiring applicability in two different ways, to denote and, alternatively, to mention-select.

That the same terms are thus used for two different functions serves to tie together the things we recognize and the representations of these things that we acknowledge as such. It also firms up, modifies, or develops relevant general procedures of representation. That a given tree-picture is labeled "tree" works to reinforce the method by which this picture was created or interpreted as a tree-representation and to extend such mode of representation to other objects than trees. It also encourages the perception of objects with the peculiar emphases accorded them by the representations in question. A revolutionary new process of picturing trees reverberates throughout our procedures of representation, affecting our view of other represented objects as well. The learning of terms, null or not, proceeds by a variety of routes, passing through representations of diverse interlocking sorts, as well as searching for denotata of the terms themselves. This is the force of the statement that opened this chapter, that is, the statement that we live in a world of symbols as well as other things.

2 RITUAL AND MENTION-SELECTION

In Chapter 10, we shall note the role of mention-selection in interpreting primitive mimetic identification, where ordinary mortals are identified with divine beings for the space of a rite. We shall also see mention-selection in idolatry, where an artifact is identified with a god. In both these cases, the identification is mistaken but understandable. It is mistaken, for gods are neither ordinary mortals nor artifacts. It is, however, understandable as a natural but corrigible error in which a term, correctly applied to a thing mention-selectively, is incorrectly applied to it denotatively.

To say that the identification is a natural but corrigible error is to say that it does not result from a constitutional inability to distinguish between a symbol and what it purports to apply to – for example, between an idol and the spirit it depicts. Rather, the identification wrongly interprets the fact that a symbol indubitably applies, via mention-selection, to some artifact or mortal functioning as a god-representation. Having mention-selected such representation, it proceeds to attribute to it, via denotation, properties appropriate only to the god that is its purported object. In a related example of identification, a mimetic gesture portrays the act of a god and purports, in this role, to be denotative. But it also mention-selects representations of the same act, itself included. Then, by confusion of such mention-selection with denotation, the gesture in question is itself taken to be the act of a god and not just the portrayal of such an act. Analogously, the verbal description, "act of the god," mention-selects the mimetic portrayal that is, then, by the same transition to denotation, taken to be the act portrayed.

Various theorists have postulated a gross confusion of symbol with thing as either a generally ineradicable mental tendency – a disease of language – or as, at any rate, an inherent feature of the mind of the "other" – the primitive, the child, or the insane. I have, on the contrary, assumed that the tendency to the error in question is a hazard that besets everyone, but that it is, nevertheless, easy to overcome with a certain degree of care.

Earlier, I said that the erroneous identification begins by mention-selecting the symbol and ends by ascribing to it predicates appropriate only to its purported object. But the matter is hardly so clear-cut and sequential. Nor can we reasonably suppose that the contrast between denotation and mention-selection was available to awareness from the earliest times. Rather, I conjecture that, in the beginning, there was confusion of words and things, a mixture of use and mention. Anthropologists and other scholars have described in multifarious detail a variety of related phenomena – for example, attribution of causal power to words, (e.g., incantations), fears related to words (e.g., curses), ascription of potency to names. Ernst Cassirer, for example, refers to the notion of an "essential identity between the word and what it denotes" as characterizing such phenomena.[3] Alternatively, I suggest, they may perhaps be grouped under the general idea of a confusion of denotation with mention-selection, the creation of a family of representations in which each term indifferently refers to its instances and, concurrently, to its companion signs.

In this indiscriminate usage, each "tree" refers to trees but also to tree-pictures and to "tree"s. No wonder that in the child's world and the world of the primitive, for example, symbols take on some of the features and powers of extrasymbolic reality. A picture of a lion is certainly perceived as different from the live animal represented, but the picture, no less than the animal, is after all called "lion." It is thus vulnerable to the inference that it is to be feared as dangerous – the representation in this way mistakenly treated as one of its own denotata. With the eventual dawning of the fundamental distinction between denotation and mention-selection, however, come various devices for fixing it in mind – including the use of explicit compounds of terms to denote their respective ranges of mention-selection. "Picture of a tree," "tree-picture," and "tree-description," for example, come to supplant "tree" itself in reference to tree-mentions when theoretical clarity is important, and denotation alone now suffices, without mention-selection, to make the appropriate distinctions. Of course, mention-selection persists, as I have urged, but it is recognized as a function different from denotation, and it is theoretically avoidable through recourse to suitable compounds.

3 MENTION-SELECTION AND TRANSFER

Even where the relevant use of compounds has been gained, mention-selection retains its practical usefulness in defining and redefining the range of such compounds. It thereby helps to relate things to their representations, a process we have remarked on earlier. Let us now look at the process in more detail. The useful-

3 Ernst Cassirer, *Language and Myth* (New York: Dover [copyright 1946 by Harper and Brothers]), p. 49.

ness in question hinges on the referential shift of a term from what it denotes to mentions of what it purports to denote. This shift is not a matter of logical inference. It is more in the nature of a transfer phenomenon akin to metaphor. The term "elephant" does not take elephant-pictures as instances; it does not, in fact, denote them. Yet when asked to pick out the elephants in the stack of pictures before him, a subject who has earlier learned to relate other objects to their representations and who has seen live elephants will normally have no difficulty understanding the question, and little problem complying with the request. The denotative term "elephant," thus newly forced onto a given realm of pictorial mentions, will, with a surprising degree of determinacy, select (and help to define) elephant-pictures in fact. The direction of transfer here is from *denotation* to *selection*, and the items selected by the term "elephant" are in turn denoted by the compound "elephant-picture." The range of the compound is thus specified through the intermediary, transferred action of mention-selection by the term in question.

Conversely, "elephant-picture" may be transferred to real elephants, the representation helping to form a determinate and appropriate array of animals. This process may be conceived as one in which "elephant," having initially mention-selected a certain group of pictures identifiable as elephant-pictures, is then forced onto the animal realm, where no mentions are found, the request being, as before, to pick out the elephants. Here, the direction of transfer is from *selection* to *denotation*, with the denotation of instances following the lead of mention-selection, the total process helping to define the very distinction itself.

The interplay between denotation and mention-selection is mirrored in the processes by which representations are modified by acquaintance with things, and commerce with things modified by acquaintance with their representations. Thus, familiarity with objects of various sorts and facility in denoting them may be used as a base for acquiring the ability to recognize certain of their mentions. Conversely, familiarity with such mentions affects, in incalculable ways, our relations with their objects, as, for example, in the formation of stereotypes. Both processes may, further, be variously intertwined. Learning to "read" photographs, given initial recognition of the people they represent, we may then use photographs of hitherto unknown persons as aids to recognizing them upon first appearance. Learning to recognize fractured bones with the help of designated X-ray mentions of them, we may expand our competence in identifying allied representations of other disabilities.[4]

4 MENTION-SELECTION IN LITERATURE AND SCIENCE

Perfectly routine use of mention-selection is hardly noticed since it pervades our ordinary practice in various ways. We have noted the captioning of pictures by the use of terms for their purported objects. Discussions of literary representations typically involve mention-selection as well. As Elgin has remarked, "Literary critics apply terms mention-selectively when they say things like 'Hamlet was a man who couldn't make up his mind' rather than 'Hamlet-descriptions are man-who-couldn't-make-up-his-mind-descriptions'."[5] And when, during the course of a performance of "Hamlet," a member of the audience says, "There's Hamlet, coming on stage now!" he is not to be understood as merely uttering a literal falsehood; he is saying something accurate. I take his "Hamlet" utterance to be mention-selecting a Hamlet-representation, that is, the actor playing Hamlet.[6]

Elgin has also pointed out the occurrence of mention-selection in connection with the use of fictive terms in the sciences rather than in literature. She notes that "scientists use such terms as 'a perfect vacuum', 'an ideal gas', 'a free market', despite the widespread recognition that there are, properly speaking, no perfect vacuums, ideal gases, or free markets." These expressions, she argues,

---

4 This section draws on my discussion in *Beyond the Letter*, pp. 47–9.
5 Catherine Z. Elgin, *With Reference to Reference* (Indianapolis, Ind.: Hackett, 1983), p. 48.
6 Israel Scheffler, "Four Questions of Fiction," *Poetics*, 11 (1982), 279–84; reprinted in my *Inquiries* (Indianapolis, Ind.: Hackett, 1986), pp. 74–79.

function not denotively, but mention-selectively. In introducing such a term, we introduce a label that mention-selects an idealization obtained by, e.g., letting the values of certain variables go to zero. Since the values in question do not in fact, or at any rate, do not all at once, go to zero, the idealization does not describe any actual situation. Thus, in giving an account of the semantics of a theory, we are not concerned to ask, "What is an ideal gas?" for the answer to that is straightforward: nothing. We are concerned, rather, to ask, "What is an ideal-gas-description?" The answer to this is provided by one or another formulation of the ideal gas law.[7]

5 OPEN TEXTURE, ANALYTICITY, AND MENTION-SELECTION

Mention-selection provides a perspicuous way of formulating certain significant features of everyday language. Consider first what F. Waismann has described as the "open texture" of language, that is, the possibility of vagueness in its descriptive terms.[8] What is meant here is that any such term, even if free of vagueness in a given domain of objects, is potentially vague in a hypothetically enlarged domain.

Waismann imagines a catlike creature that "grew to a gigantic size . . . or could be revived from death," taking such imagined creature to show "that we can think of situations in which we couldn't be certain whether something was a cat or some other animal (or a *jinni*)."[9] The question is how to interpret Waismann's claim. There are serious difficulties in any view that takes him to be postulating a possible gigantic cat as borderline instance of "cat" in a hypothetically enlarged domain. For, in the first place, possible objects are wrapped in philosophical obscurity since

7 Elgin, *With Reference to Reference*, p. 49.
8 Friedrich Waismann, "Verifiability," *Proceedings of the Aristotelian Society*, 19(supplement) (1945), 119–50. Reprinted in A. Flew, ed., *Logic and Language* (First Series, Oxford: Blackwell, 1951; and First and Second Series, Garden City, N.Y.: Anchor Books, 1965), pp. 122–51.
9 Ibid., (Anchor Books edition), p. 125.

they lack a clear principle of individuation. And in the second place, since a *possible* cat is no cat at all, "cat" is not, after all, undecided relative to a *possible* gigantic cat and hence not vague in the hypothetically enlarged domain in question.

However, Waismann's claim can be interpreted, not in terms of *possible borderline objects,* but rather in terms of actual representations (e.g., pictures, descriptions) of relevant sorts. Having mastered the use of "cat" in application to familiar things, we may yet be undecided as to whether to apply "picture of a cat" to the painting of a catlike creature depicted as standing higher than the Empire State Building or, what comes to the same thing, whether or not to caption the painting "cat." A child may be baffled as to whether or not to caption the picture of a zebra "horse," using the latter term not to denote, but to select horse-mentions.

Open texture may now be seen to depend not on the hypothetical expansion of a term's given domain or its putative reference to possible objects, but rather on the uncertainty with which its mention-denoting compounds apply to actual things. That is, every descriptive term has some compound with "-picture" or "-description" or "-representation," which in each case is vague relative to some domain. More simply yet, Waismann's thesis comes to this: Every descriptive term is uncertain with respect to its mention-selection of some actual object.

Consider now the much discussed question of *analyticity* in everyday language, or, in a related idiom, the question of which of its statements are necessary, and which merely contingent. We have seen how to interpret open texture through reference to actual representations. A similar interpretation may now be suggested for analyticity. For the questions of (1) whether or not there is a *possible* cat that stands four stories high, (2) whether a cat *might* stand four stories high, (3) whether it is just *contingently* true that no cat stands four stories high (and not *necessarily* so), and (4) whether, in particular, it is only *synthetic* rather than *analytic* that cats do not stand four stories high might all be understood as asking whether certain descriptions, pictures, or other mentions are cat-representations or not.

For example, a subject's willingness to call "animal shaped like a cat but standing four stories high" a cat-description would count in favor of an affirmative attitude to the four preceding questions; the subject's unwillingness would be held to indicate a negative attitude. More simply, a subject's willingness to take "cat" as mention-selecting the above description would be taken as a positive, while an unwillingness would be taken as a negative, response. That is, a willingness to label the preceding description as indeed a description of a cat would be an indication that he or she affirms a possible cat's standing four stories high, thinks a cat might stand four stories high, holds it to be merely contingently, and not necessarily, true that no cat stands four stories high, and holds this fact to be synthetic only, and not analytic.

In general, a subject's mention-selective habits relative to a given term might be said to represent his or her division of true statements involving the term into analytic and synthetic truths. And open texture – that is, the uncertainty or ambivalence of these habits in application to some object – would reflect a gap in such division. The thesis of universal open texture we have earlier discussed can now be seen to imply that every term is such that the true statements in which it figures cannot be exhaustively divided into analytic and synthetic truths for any subject. The upshot is that the analytic–synthetic distinction, as earlier interpreted, is always incomplete.

Mention-selective transfer of a term involves the shift of such a term, say "horse," from what it denotes, that is, horses, to appropriate parallel representations, that is, horse-pictures. Such a shift is akin to the metaphorical extension of linguistic habits. This helps to explain the variability in judgments of analyticity. Taken out of the realm of logical inference or quasi-logical intuition and reinterpreted in terms of metaphorical, psychological, and pedagogical transfer, the traditional philosophical problem of analyticity is replaced by inquiries into the subtle interactions of mention-selection and denotation in the course of learning and subsequent symbolic practice.[10]

10 The foregoing section draws on my discussion in *Beyond the Letter* (London: Routledge, 1979), pp. 51–7.

Section II
Symbol and ambiguity

Chapter 3
Ambiguity in language

What is ambiguity? Under what conditions is a word ambiguous? We all claim a certain practical facility in spotting ambiguities, but the theory of the matter is in a sorry state. Logicians and philosophers typically concern themselves with ambiguity either as a defect in the arguments of others or as a hazard from which their own serious discourse is to be protected. Literary critics, alive to the rhetorical values of ambiguous expression, are not equally sensitive to the philosophical demands for clarity and system. General analytical questions thus remain for the most part unexplored, while commonly repeated explanations suffer from various grave difficulties.

A word is, for example, said to be ambiguous if it has different meanings or senses, or if it stands for different ideas. But ghostly entities such as meanings, senses, or ideas provide no more than the ghost of an explanation unless, as seems unlikely, they can be clearly construed as countable things whose relations to one another and to words are independently determinable. At best, such entities may be regarded as hypostatizations of the content of sets of synonymous expressions, the specification resting on the critically obscure notion of synonymy.

"Ambiguity in Language" appeared as "Ambiguity: An Inscriptional Approach" in Richard Rudner and Israel Scheffler, eds., *Logic and Art: Essays in Honor of Nelson Goodman* (Indianapolis, Ind.: Bobbs-Merrill, 1972, now Atascadero, Calif.: Ridgeview), pp. 251–72.

In a more concrete vein, a word may be said to be ambiguous in having different dictionary readings, that is, in being correlated with different actual expressions in the dictionary. But which dictionary is to be chosen and how has it been composed? Are the principles by which its readings have been assigned clearly formulable; can we be confident that they themselves make no appeal to the lexicographer's unanalyzed judgments of ambiguity?

Further, we must ask in what the relevant difference of readings consists. Presumably, they are to be not merely different but nonsynonymous; the proposed criterion of ambiguity thus presupposes, without providing an answer to the troublesome question of synonymy. Alternatively, it may be suggested that we consider not different actual expressions, but different abstract readings, a reading to be construed now as an intensional entity correlated with a set of synonymous expressions; the individuation of readings again hinges on synonymy, and the postulation of such purported entities takes us back to meanings or senses once more.

Moreover, the criterion at best falls short of providing a sufficient condition, for nonsynonymous readings, however construed, may signify generality rather than ambiguity. For the word "caravan," for instance, we find the following two readings:[1]

(i) a group of travelers journeying together through desert or hostile regions.
(ii) a group of vehicles traveling together in a file.

Is it clear that these two readings signify the ambiguity of "caravan" rather than mark out two regions of its general, and unambiguous, application?

Finally, are the expressions representing the readings themselves assumed to be purified of ambiguity? Unless they are, we cannot take the lack of nonsynonymous readings for a given word to betoken its freedom from ambiguity. On the other hand,

---

1 *The New Merriam–Webster Pocket Dictionary* (New York: Pocket Books, G. & C. Merriam, 1964), p. 72.

to require the readings themselves to be unambiguous renders the criterion, as a whole, circular.

1 ELEMENTARY AMBIGUITY (E-AMBIGUITY)

The proposals just considered have this in common: Between words and denoted things, they interpose additional entities as the root of ambiguity – meanings or senses or ideas or readings – entities whose individuation or explanatory role is obscure, involving, at the very least, appeal to the controverted notion of synonymy. Can any progress be made by wiping the slate clean, renouncing such interposition altogether and restricting ourselves to words and ordinary things? In fact, will an inscriptional approach, considering word-tokens only and surrendering the notion of associated abstract types, enable us to advance the analysis of ambiguity? Such an approach has advantages that have shown themselves in other problem areas,[2] and it has one basic advantage: that the entities it requires are also acknowledged by other approaches, so that it presupposes nothing controversial for itself.

A simplified inscriptional account may be sketched as follows: We treat written tokens only and, among these, attend only to predicate tokens. These, however, are given to us embedded in naturally occurring contexts, which enable us, generally, to judge certain of their denotative relations. Then, for any two predicate tokens x and y, we ask:

(i) Are x and y spelled exactly alike, that is, are they replicas of one another?

(ii) Are x and y extensionally divergent, that is, does either one denote something not denoted by the other?

2 See, e.g., Nelson Goodman and Willard Van Orman Quine, "Steps Toward a Constructive Nominalism," *Journal of Symbolic Logic,* 12 (1947), 105–22; Chap. 11 of Nelson Goodman, *The Structure of Appearance,* 2nd ed. (Indianapolis, Ind.: Bobbs-Merrill, 1966); Israel Scheffler, *The Anatomy of Inquiry* (New Nork: Knopf, 1963), Part I, secs. 6 and 8.

Given tokens x and y for which the answers to these questions are both positive, we now say they are ambiguous with respect to one another. Further, given simply x, we hold it ambiguous if there is some token y with respect to which it is ambiguous.

This account needs, of course, to be relativized to a discourse D to become effective, for, as it stands, it characterizes x as ambiguous if it has an extensionally divergent replica in some other language or remote context. The condition it sets is far too weak and, hence, satisfied by vastly more (perhaps all) predicate tokens than are ordinarily deemed ambiguous. That x fulfills this condition is compatible with its being perfectly unambiguous within the space of some restricted discourse of interest. We thus amplify the account by adding that x is ambiguous within a containing discourse D if and only if x belongs to D and is ambiguous with respect to some token within D.

The proposal just sketched is, to be sure, limited. It restricts itself to predicate tokens and does not deal with other sorts of word-tokens or with word-sequences of sentence length or more. It gives no account of syntactic ambiguities, but treats only ambiguity of a semantic sort. Yet it covers an undeniably important variety, of the same sort with which we have, in fact, been concerned from the beginning and earlier accounts of which we found wanting in our previous discussion. We shall refer to the present proposal as providing an *elementary (inscriptional) notion of ambiguity.*

2 ASPECTS OF ELEMENTARY AMBIGUITY

The idea of the above proposal is set forth by Nelson Goodman from the point of view of a primary interest in indicator terms:

> Roughly speaking, a word is an *indicator* if . . . it names something not named by some replica of the word. This is admittedly broad, including ambiguous terms as well as what might be regarded as indicators-proper, such as pronouns; but

delimitation of the narrower class of indicators-proper is a ticklish business and is not needed for our present purposes.[3]

The inclusive category is, from the point of view of our present concerns, that of *ambiguity*, with indicators forming one subgroup of ambiguous terms, roughly distinguishable by the fact that extensional variation across indicator-replicas is related, in a relatively simple, systematic manner, to some contextual feature of these replicas. Thus, an "I" normally refers to its own producer and a "now" to a suitable time period within which its own production lies. Another subgroup is constituted by metaphorical terms, a metaphorical predicate within *D* roughly characterizable as having therein some replica with divergent extension related to its own in special ways, the latter literal counterpart providing, in some manner, a clue to application of the former.

Elementary ambiguity, as explained earlier, is distinguishable from generality in that a token ambiguous within *D* must diverge extensionally from some replica therein. If no such divergence exists, the fact that a token applies to many things signifies only that it is general, no matter how dissimilar these things may be, by whatever criteria of similarity may be chosen. That a "table" denotes big as well as little tables argues not its ambiguity but only its breadth of applicability. Though difficult to apply in certain instances, the distinction will nevertheless be effective in many others. In the sentence "This book contains a table of contents on page 4," the constituent "table" token diverges extensionally from replicas denoting items of furniture. Philosophical disputes as to whether some critical term, for example, "exists," *should* be construed as ambiguous, or merely general, hinge on theoretical considerations. The problem of settling the construction of a term for special theoretical purposes is different, however, from that of judging the issue of ambiguity versus generality as affecting ordinary terms within given discourses. At any rate, the purport of even the philosophical issue may be clarified by the distinction.

3 Goodman, *The Structure of Appearance*, p. 362.

Elementary ambiguity will also be distinguishable from vagueness, where the latter is taken to involve a certain indeterminacy or ambivalence in deciding the applicability of a term to an object. For x, within D, may be unambiguous and yet vague relative to some object o, all its replicas within D being alike indeterminate respecting o. Conversely, x and y may be ambiguous with respect to one another within D, neither displaying vagueness relative to any o within our domain of consideration. Indicators provide the most striking, if not the only, examples, each of several "I" tokens within a given D being, we may imagine, clearly decidable in its denotation, which yet varies from that of each other replica within D.

Elementary ambiguity, therefore, does not altogether accord with usual understandings. It consists in extensional variation among replicas, each of which may, however, be perfectly definite in the way we apply it. Reverting to the language of types, we may say it is a feature of variability of the type rather than a species of variability characterizing the single token; moreover, type variability may occasion no problem of decision. On the other hand, we often convey, in calling an expression "ambiguous," that there is some difficulty attaching to its interpretation in a given occurrence, some indecision infecting the single token. Such a point has been often noted. Hospers, for example, writes, "Sometimes, in fact, the very word 'ambiguity' is restricted so as to mean only *misleading* ambiguity."[4] Richman distinguishes "semantical ambiguity," as the possession of more than one meaning by an expression, from "psychological ambiguity," as the occurrence of a semantically ambiguous expression in a context in which the intended interpretation is unclear.[5] Quine remarks that "ambiguity is supposed to consist in indecisiveness between meanings."[6] Having here renounced the notion of meanings, can

---

4 John Hospers, *An Introduction to Philosophical Analysis* (New York: Prentice-Hall, 1953), p. 23. Cited in R. J. Richman, "Ambiguity and Intuition," *Mind*, 68 (1959), 87.
5 Ibid., and see the footnote, p. 87, where the point is credited to Bertram Jessup.
6 Willard Van Orman Quine, *Word and Object* (New York: Technology Press of MIT and Wiley, 1960), p. 132.

we account for indecision with respect to the individual token, a feature not implied by elementary ambiguity in itself?

To assimilate such indecision to mere vagueness would miss the crucial point that, as Richman puts it, "psychological ambiguity involves semantical ambiguity";[7] the indecision affecting the given token must be related to the fact that its type is ambiguous. But we have already mirrored type variability in the notion of elementary ambiguity, so our problem is to relate the indecision in question here to elementary ambiguity. Suppose then that z and y are replicas of x and extensionally divergent and, hence, ambiguous with respect to one another within discourse D containing both; let us, moreover, take D as also containing x. Now assume x embedded in a context that does not rule out its being extensionally equivalent either to z or to y. Let us, to simplify the example, also bar from D any further replica of x that is not extensionally equivalent either to z or to y. Now, to interpret x as extensionally equivalent to z or to y will enable a clear decision regarding x's extension. Either of these interpretations makes good sense of the relevant embedding context and, we may imagine, is simpler or is more convenient than the assignment to x of a wholly new extension that makes equal sense. Either interpretation will enable us to understand what attribution is accomplished in the context in question by the presence of x. Yet we cannot in fact find sufficient reason in this situation to make up our minds, for the alternative decisions are equally reasonable. Note that if x is a predicate token attached to the name of an object o, our indecision relates not to the fact that o is said to fall within the extension of x, but rather to what the application of x accomplishes, that is, what x's extension is: Is o, in particular, asserted to fall within the extension of z or of y? Here is an inscriptional example, readily generalizable, of what Quine calls "indecisiveness between meanings," the indecision being a matter of aligning x with one or another divergent replica, each providing in itself a definite clue to a plausible interpretation.[8] Where x is

7 Richman, "Ambiguity and Intuition," p. 87.
8 The interpretation here proposed accords with the notion that ambiguity of occurrence presupposes "semantical ambiguity." Of course, there may be anal-

characterized by such indecision, we shall describe it as I-ambiguous (relative to context c).

3 A NEW PROBLEM: GREEN CENTAURS

So far, elementary ambiguity has been offered as an account of so-called type variability, and "ambiguity of occurrence" has been explained by elementary ambiguity coupled with an appeal to the relative richness of a token's available context. Is this the whole story?

Richman notes the following case, which presents us with a new problem. "'Green centaur'," he writes, "is an ambiguous term since it may be used to mean centaurs of a certain color, or centaurs of a certain degree of experience; the classes referred to, however, are both identical, both being empty."[9] Now imagine any two English "green centaur" tokens x and y. Though replicas, they are not extensionally divergent, and so lack elementary ambiguity. Faced, moreover, with such an unlikely sentence as

> In my dream I met some experienced zebras and a green centaur,

if we cannot decide which interpretation to place upon the "green centaur" token, it is no longer open to us to explain our indecision as we earlier dealt with ambiguity of occurrence. For we there required replicas of the undecided token with divergent extensions, whereas every replica of our undecided "green centaur" token, within our operative domain, has the same (null) extension. Thus, we cannot suppose our present indecision to be a matter of aligning some token with one or another replica with divergent extensions.[10] If, moreover, we find two sentences with sufficient context to resolve the indecision in question, say,

ogous cases where indecision concerns the alignment of x with divergent non-replicas of appropriate sort.

9 Richman, "Ambiguity and Intuition," p. 88.

10 Indeed, the two interpretations in question are themselves coextensive, so the indecision cannot be attributed to variable extension, independently of whether or not divergent replicas are available.

(i) There were a yellow griffin, a purple unicorn, and a green centaur at the tea party,

and

(ii) Though most of the centaurs present were well schooled in the social graces, there was also one green centaur, whose inexperience made him visibly uncomfortable,

we still need to account for our interpreting the "green centaur" token in (i) as differing in meaning from its replica in (ii), despite their extensional equivalence. In what does their unlikeness of meaning consist, failing elementary ambiguity?

It is worth noting here that the general problem of likeness of meaning (or synonymy) is the converse of the problem of ambiguity. The former concerns the conditions under which two words have the same meaning, while the latter concerns the conditions under which the same word has different meanings. While the first asks when two words have the same meaning, the second, we may say, asks when two meanings have the same word. In discussing the first problem, Nelson Goodman reached the conclusion that no two words have the same meaning, but he was considering words as types.[11] Further discussions of his ideas in papers by Richard Rudner, Beverly Robbins, and Goodman deal with the extension of these ideas to tokens.[12] Since the problem of ambiguity is the reverse of that of likeness of meaning, it will be worth seeing if the inscriptional extension referred to bears on our present problem. We shall find that it does, and in unexpected ways.

4 DIFFERENCE IN MEANING

In dealing with ambiguity, we made some progress through appeal to extensional divergence but encountered difficulty in cases

11 Nelson Goodman, "On Likeness of Meaning," *Analysis,* 10 (1949), 1–7.
12 R. Rudner, "A Note on Likeness of Meaning," *Analysis,* 10 (1950) 115–18; B. L. Robbins, "On Synonymy of Word-Events," *Analysis,* 12 (1952), 98–100; N. Goodman, "On Some Differences About Meaning," *Analysis,* 13, (1953), 90–6.

where ambiguity persists without such divergence. Sameness of extension, we saw, does not in every case remove differences of meaning associated with different replicas. A parallel inadequacy forms the main problem to which Goodman's "On Likeness of Meaning" is addressed: Sameness of extension does not guarantee sameness of meaning in the case of *words*, that is, types. The words "centaur" and "unicorn," for example, differ in meaning though not in extension.

To account for this fact, Goodman proposes that it is not only the extensions of the original two words themselves that we need to consider (so-called *primary* extensions), but also the extensions of their parallel compounds (so-called *secondary* extensions). A pair of parallel compounds is formed by making an identical addition to each of the two words under consideration; thus, adding "picture" to "centaur" and "unicorn," we have the parallel pair "centaur-picture" and "unicorn-picture." Now, although there are neither centaurs nor unicorns, there certainly are centaur-pictures and unicorn-pictures, and moreover, they are different. Though the original words have the same extension, the parallel compounds differ in extension. Goodman's idea is, then, that the difference in meaning between two words is a matter of either their own difference in extension or that of any of their parallel compounds. Terms, in general, have the same meaning if and only if they have the same primary and secondary extensions.

The proposal is further generalized to cover cases in which the addition of "picture" yields a term with null extension; for example, "acrid-odor-picture" and "pungent-odor-picture" have the same (null) extension since neither applies to anything. Compounds can, however, be formed by other additions, and Goodman argues that "description" constitutes a suffix capable of yielding all the wanted distinctions for every pair of words P and Q. For any actual inscription of the form "a P that is not a Q" is a physical thing denoted by the compound "P-description," but not by the parallel compound "Q-description." And any inscription of "a Q that is not a P" belongs to the extension of "Q-description" but not to that of "P-description." Thus, "pungent-odor-description" and "acrid-odor-description" differ extensionally

34

since the first, but not the second, applies to any inscription of the form "a pungent odor that is not an acrid odor," and vice versa. Thus, even if all pungent odors are acrid and acrid odors pungent, the terms "pungent odor" and "acrid odor" differ in meaning. It follows from this proposal, in fact, that "no two different words have the same meaning."[13]

Goodman's paper was intended to eliminate reference to images, meanings, concepts, possibilities, and the like, and to appeal only to the notion of extension or application to physical things. But the bearers of extension he there took to be terms, that is, word-types, although, as he later acknowledged, wishing any final formulation of his doctrine to countenance only actual inscriptions or events, that is, what are commonly called "tokens." What, indeed, would be the result of extending his proposal explicitly to tokens? Would it, in particular, follow that no two tokens have the same meaning? This would, we may note, be even a stronger conclusion than the one suggested earlier by the "green centaur" example. For what the latter showed was that there are instances in which replicas differ in meaning even when they have the same extension. The stronger conclusion that no two tokens have the same meaning under any circumstances clearly goes beyond the moral of the green centaurs. It implies that there is a type ambiguity that always remains even after elementary ambiguity is eliminated. Does this stronger conclusion, however, follow from Goodman's proposal reformulated for tokens?

Rudner argues that it does. In statement *S*, "A rose is a rose," the fifth token but not the second is denoted by the term "PS5," defined as "rose-description occurring in the fifth place in *S*." It follows, says Rudner, that the second and the fifth tokens are different terms, but then, since Goodman concludes that different terms cannot have the same meaning, these tokens must differ in meaning, though they are replicas of one another.[14]

13 Goodman, "On Likeness of Meaning," p. 6. In "On Some Differences About Meaning," Goodman proposes other, and more easily applicable compounds to the same effect, e.g., "literal English _____ word."
14 Rudner, "A Note on Likeness of Meaning," p. 116.

Now, the preceding argument is vulnerable to the following criticism: While it indeed shows the first "rose" token and the second "rose" token in *S* to be different entities, it does not show that they constitute different terms or words, which would be required for them to instantiate Goodman's generalization that different *words* never have the same meaning. Rudner argues, to be sure, that "PS5" is prima facie a predicate of words, not mere tokens, but this seems hardly to the point. It is not the prima facie application of "PS5" that is decisive here, but rather whether the two "rose" tokens in question can be shown to fall under Goodman's generalization, through satisfying the specific considerations upon which it is itself based. This generalization, formulated for word-types, results after all from a special argument concerning primary and secondary extensions. The question is, therefore, not whether tokens are sometimes called "words," but rather whether this special argument can be extended to the case of tokens by independent considerations. Such considerations are, however, not offered by Rudner. He remarks that "if one takes simply the position that inscriptions and parts of inscriptions are meaningful, one can maintain that no 'repetitive' inscription [such as "A rose is a rose"] is analytic; for no two of its constituent parts have the same primary and secondary extensions."[15] The latter point is, however, not demonstrated by his argument. It shows that a third predicate, "PS5," has one but not the other of his "rose" tokens in *its* extension, but it gives no reason to suppose that these two tokens themselves do not have identical extensions, both primary and secondary.

A criticism of Rudner's paper was offered by Beverly Robbins,[16] who argued not only that Rudner had failed to deduce his strong conclusion from Goodman's proposal regarding word-types, but also that the strong conclusion does not, in fact, follow. Commenting on the passage from Rudner just quoted, to the effect that no two tokens have the same primary and secondary extensions, she raises the critical question as to the existence of relevant compounds in the case of tokens, the compounds being

15 Ibid., p. 117.
16 Robbins, "On Synonymy of Word-Events."

required for an assessment of secondary extension. Reference to secondary extension is, in turn, crucial, for, since two tokens may obviously have the same primary extension, the strong thesis that no two tokens have the same meaning depends on their never having the same secondary extensions. And this, as suggested, depends on the extensional divergence of some of their parallel compounds. But what compounds are available in the case of tokens?

Unlike a word-type, whose compounds can always be supposed (on classical Platonistic assumptions) to exist, a compound of a concrete token cannot be assumed to exist; the abstract word-type is repeatable whereas the token is not. If two tokens

> themselves are to be constituents of the compounds, then they must actually exist or have existed as so many marks or sounds within these compounds. . . . In general, if we stipulate that the compounds corresponding to two predicate-events [tokens] be formed by additions to the predicate-events themselves, then most predicate-events, being uncompounded, will lack secondary extension. Among such predicate-events, those with identical primary extensions will be synonymous, since they will also have the same secondary extensions by virtue of having none.

Robbins thus concludes that strictly to apply Goodman's criterion of likeness of meaning to tokens yields too many synonymous pairs, "e.g. any uncompounded 'centaur'-event and 'unicorn'-event, will have the same meaning."[17]

However, we can construe the compounding of a token not as its literal embeddedness within a larger token, but rather as the embeddedness of any of its replicas therein. As Robbins puts it, we can take the statement (for tokens I_1 and C_1):

> I_1 occurs in the compound C_1.

as saying:

> Some replica of I_1 is part of some replica of C_1.

17 Ibid., p. 99.

Such a construal obviates the difficulty that every "centaur" token that is not literally a part of some compound must be said to have the same meaning as every such "unicorn" token. For we can assume, or construct at will, a suitable compound, say a "centaur-picture" token containing a "centaur" replica as constituent, and we can equally assume or construct a "unicorn-picture" token containing a "unicorn" replica as constituent. The extensional divergence of these latter compound tokens would now show a difference of meaning not only between their actual first word-constituents, but also between every replica of one such constituent and every replica of the other. For by Robbins's extended notion of "occurrence within a compound," every token occurs within every compound of which it has a replica as a constituent.

By this extended notion, however, every two tokens that are replicas of each other occur in exactly the same compounds, the *replica* relation being reflexive, symmetric, and transitive. "Consequently," concludes Robbins, "if two such predicate-events have the same primary extension, they will also have the same secondary extensions. The two 'rose'-events in Rudner's example 'A rose is a rose' will, contrary to his contention, have the same meaning."[18] Commenting upon the Rudner–Robbins exchange in a later paper, Goodman concluded that the application of his thesis to tokens indeed does not yield the strong result that every two tokens differ in meaning, but "only that every two word-events [tokens] that are not replicas of each other differ in meaning."[19]

5 IMPLICATIONS FOR OUR NEW PROBLEM

To say that no two words have the same meaning is a denial of synonymy. To say, further, that no two tokens have the same meaning is an affirmation of an ambiguity so strong as to infect *all* replica-pairs whatever. Such an affirmation would account for our "green centaur" example by bringing it under a universal generalization: Two "green centaur" tokens differ in meaning

18 Ibid., p. 100.
19 Goodman, "On Some Differences about Meaning," p. 92.

simply because every two tokens differ in meaning. In generalizing ambiguity for all token-pairs, however, such an account fails to explain what is *peculiar* to our "green centaur" example, namely, that just those "green centaur" replicas that involve differing interpretations are thought to differ in meaning: Two such replicas, *both* construed as indicating centaur color, will *not* be taken to differ in meaning, whereas a pair in which one indicates color and the other degree of experience *will* be supposed to involve difference in meaning. The "green centaur" example, in other words, presents us with *particular* replica-pairs that differ in meaning even though they lack elementary ambiguity. To say that every two tokens differ in meaning is too strong a thesis to explain the particular ambiguity constituting our problem.

We have seen that this strong thesis cannot be supposed to follow from Goodman's criterion. What is the state of our problem, however, if we accept Robbins's arguments? Given two replicas with identical primary extension, they cannot diverge in secondary extension since they occur in the very same compounds. It follows that every two replicas with the same primary extension *must* have the same meaning; sameness of meaning for replicas depends solely upon sameness of primary extension. And this conclusion is in direct conflict with our "green centaur" case. For here we have replicas identical in primary extension, yet different in meaning. The situation thus turns out to be more complicated than had been supposed. Given replicas with the same primary extension, we can say neither (with Rudner) that every two of them differ in meaning, nor (with Robbins) that every two of them are alike in meaning. Some such pairs show sameness whereas some show difference. But on what does this variation depend?

6 DERIVATIVE CONSTITUENT AMBIGUITY

One answer that suggests itself immediately is to take into account the extensions of word-constituents as well as compounds. Goodman's original criterion hinged on reference to the extensions of the two original words themselves, as well as to the extensions of their compounds. Applied to tokens, this criterion (as we have seen) cannot account for the "green centaur" case. But we need only note here that replicas of the word-constituent "green" are characterized by elementary ambiguity, since some denote things of a certain color and others denote things of a certain degree of experience. Moreover, the particular difference of meaning between those "green centaur" tokens involving differing interpretations is exactly associated with difference of extensional assignment to the constituent "green" tokens in question. What is suggested, then, is a revision of Goodman's original criterion to include reference to word-constituents: Tokens are alike in meaning if and only if they have the same primary extensions, the same secondary extensions, and the same constituent extensions, where the latter clause is to be taken as requiring the same primary extensions for parallel word-constituents.[20]

In *Languages of Art*, Goodman suggests such a revision of his criterion as applied to sign-types, for independent reasons, namely, because restricted artificial languages may bar the free compounding characteristic of natural languages. Discussing his original criterion, he writes:

> As applied to natural languages, where there is great freedom in generating compounds, this criterion tends to give the result that every two terms differ in meaning. No such result follows for more restricted languages; and indeed for these the criterion may need to be strengthened by providing further that characters differ in meaning if they are parallel compounds of terms that differ either in primary or in parallel secondary extension.[21]

20 The constituent extensions need to be primary only, for in the case of tokens with which we are here concerned, secondary extensions differentiate only among nonreplicas, but if parallel constituents are nonreplicas, the wholes will also be nonreplicas, and thus already distinguished by the earlier reference to secondary extensions of the wholes. On the other hand, where the wholes are replicas, and also have the same primary extensions, they may be distinguished through the varying primary extensions of their parallel word-constituents.

21 Nelson Goodman, *Languages of Art* (Indianapolis, Ind.: Bobbs-Merrill, 1968), p. 205, n. 16. Secondary extensions of constituents are here included, since the context concerns types rather than tokens. (See n. 20, this chapter.)

The motivation for the proposal in this passage is to provide a suitable criterion for restricted languages, whereas our present motivation has been to take account of meaning differences among replicas, which share all their compounds. But the common general point is the need for a strengthening of the original criterion when limitations of one or another sort are placed on compounding. For word-types in languages with structural restrictions on compounding, reference to constituents is thus indicated. For tokens, where compounds of replicas are shared by all such replicas, and where compounding is thus powerless to differentiate among them, reference to constituents is equally indicated.

Once we take constituents into account, we can deal with the sort of ambiguity represented by the "green centaur" case, a case not dealt with by Robbins's treatment. She treats replicas with identical primary extension, arguing that they cannot differ in secondary extension, that is, cannot occur in parallel compounds with divergent extension. Our "green centaur" case offers replicas with identical primary extension, but containing parallel constituents with differing primary extension. We have here, in other words, compounds lacking elementary ambiguity, but containing constituents possessing elementary ambiguity. We can thus now acknowledge, in extensional terms, the peculiar difference of meaning among certain compound replicas that have the same primary extensions. This sort of difference of meaning we shall refer to as *derivative constituent ambiguity*. Moreover, corresponding to the latter, which is another form of type variability, we may also note a new sort of "ambiguity of occurrence," involving indecision as to the interpretation of a single token, whose context is too meager to settle the extensional alignment of a constituent; this concept is parallel to that of our earlier notion of ambiguity of occurrence related to elementary ambiguity of the whole.

7 DERIVATIVE COMPOUND AMBIGUITY

A critical case remains yet to be considered, one that is beyond the reach of any of the notions so far developed. Consider first that derivative constituent ambiguity depends upon the separability of word-constituents of given tokens. Can we not conceive of an ambiguity that remains even when such separability is not allowed? Imagine, for example, that every "green centaur" token has been learned initially as a single indivisible unit, and that no mastery of isolated "green" tokens has as yet been gained. It is, however, known that all "greencentaur" tokens are identical in extension, there being no greencentaurs. Thus, there is here no elementary ambiguity, nor is there, for lack of relevant separability, any derivative constituent ambiguity. (There can, further, be no ambiguity of occurrence in any of the forms so far distinguished.) Nevertheless, a form of ambiguity persists: The situation is here strikingly different from that involving, say, just "unicorn" tokens, which also lack elementary as well as derivative constituent ambiguity. What is this difference?

The contrast is seen immediately if we form compounds with "picture" tokens in each case. All "unicorn-picture" tokens have the same extension; on the other hand, "all greencentaur-picture" tokens are marked by elementary ambiguity: Some of these denote what, from a more sophisticated standpoint, might be described as green-colored-centaur-pictures (or pictures of green-colored centaurs), whereas others denote what, from the same standpoint, might be described as immature-centaur-pictures (or pictures of immature centaurs), irrespective of the purported color of the depicted centaur. Given what sophisticates might describe as a picture of a green-colored but worldly wise centaur or a picture of a yellow, baby centaur, it will be denoted by some but not all of the "greencentaur-picture" replicas. The point, in short, is this: Even though indivisible "greencentaur" tokens *lack* elementary ambiguity, certain of their compounds, for example, "greencentaur-picture" tokens, *do possess* elementary ambiguity.

Nor does this general sort of case depend upon our imagined circumstance in which the constituent of a compound ("green" in "greencentaur") has not yet been grasped as a separable unit. Suppose two novelists use the same name "Algernon" for their central characters in two fictional works. All replicas of the name within our given domain may then have the same (null) extension, and there are no word-constituents in any of these replicas.

Yet "Algernon-description" tokens may display elementary ambiguity, some denoting portions of the one fictional work, and others denoting portions of the other. Myths employ the same name for purportedly different but actually nonexistent characters. Thus, "The child Linus of Argos must be distinguished from Linus, the son of Ismenius, whom Heracles killed with a lyre."[22] And Argus, the hound; Argus, son of Medea; Argus Panoptes; and Argus the Thespian are all to be distinguished despite the sharing of a name with null extension and no word-constituents.[23]

Recalling Robbins's argument against the efficacy of secondary extensions to distinguish among replicas with identical primary extension, we find that she does not make this critical contrast between compounds *with,* and compounds *without,* elementary ambiguity. Concerning the two "rose" tokens in a given "A rose is a rose," she argues that they must occur in exactly the same compounds, since to occur in a compound (by her extended notion) is to have a replica therein. Thus, given a compound containing a replica of the one "rose" token, this compound must also contain a replica of the other, the replica relation being transitive. "Consequently," she concludes, "if two such predicate-events have the same primary extension, they will also have the same secondary extensions."[24]

Now, in any case, replicas have the same secondary extensions. But such *sameness* of secondary extension does not imply that the extensions of the relevant compounds are the *same.* The compounds, although *shared* by all replicas of the constituents, may themselves *diverge* in extension, that is, possess elementary ambiguity. The example Robbins deals with is one in which the relevant compounds ("rose-description" tokens) do not suggest such ambiguity, but the possibility of such ambiguity is nevertheless clear.

Consider, for example, replicas (unlike "rose" tokens) that

22 Robert Graves, *The Greek Myths* (New York: Braziller, 1957), Vol. 2, p. 212, sec. 147.
23 Ibid.
24 Robbins, "On Synonymy of Word-Events," p. 100.

differ in primary extension, for example, two tokens T_1 and T_2, of the word "trunk," T_1 denoting containers of a certain sort and T_2 denoting certain portions of elephants. Since they are replicas, T_1 and T_2 have exactly the same secondary extensions, but such sameness clearly does not preclude elementary ambiguity of compound "trunk-picture" tokens, some of which denote certain container-pictures but not elephant-pictures, while some do just the reverse. Since T_1 and T_2 differ in primary extension, they ipso facto differ in meaning, so that consideration of their compounds is, for Robbins's purposes, superfluous. But the question that concerns us here is this: Given indivisible replicas with *identical* primary extensions, does the elementary ambiguity of their shared secondary extension contribute a new form of derivative ambiguity to the original replicas? The "rose" example, to be sure, does not highlight this problem, but the examples introduced in the present section do raise the issue. The "greencentaur-picture" tokens, the "Algernon-description" tokens, the "Linus-description" tokens, and the "Argus-description" tokens display elementary ambiguity in spite of the lack of elementary ambiguity of their respective constituents. We thus have here, it seems, another form of ambiguity, flowing inward to the constituent from elementary ambiguity of the compound; we shall refer to it as *derivative compound ambiguity*.

8 MENTION-SELECTION

Derivative compound ambiguity diverges, in a critical manner, from forms hitherto recognized: It fails to correlate differing extensions differentially with the ambiguous replicas in question. That is, given replicas R_1 and R_2, if they possess elementary ambiguity, they themselves differ in extension, while if they have derivative constituent ambiguity, some constituent of R_1 differs in extension from a parallel constituent of R_2. For derivative compound ambiguity, we cannot say the same thing. To be sure, the compounds of R_1 and R_2 differ in extension, but these divergent compounds cannot be differentially assigned to R_1 and R_2, for the latter two replicas occur in all the *very same* compounds, by Robbins's criterion.

44

It is true that extensional variation among compounds, which is here in question, has already shown itself significant in the case of nonreplicas: Learning the difference in meaning between a "centaur" token and a "unicorn" token is *not* learning to associate different extensions with the latter pair or with their respective parallel constituents. Rather it is to learn to differentiate centaur-pictures from unicorn-pictures, centaur-descriptions from unicorn-descriptions, and so forth. But then, if learning the word "centaur" is learning how to apply also "centaur-picture," for example, then learning the indivisible word "greencentaur" is learning how to apply "greencentaur-picture" as well. And if the latter is plagued by elementary ambiguity, how can learning proceed coherently? If a child correctly withholds the term "centaur" from everything, it may still not be clear whether he is capable of correctly selecting centaur-pictures, and until he can do this we may be unwilling to admit that he has gotten the whole point. Where elementary ambiguity infects the compounds, there are, so to speak, two or more points to be gotten. We may, by subsidiary indication, help to resolve the ambiguity, limiting relevant compounds (in teaching) to certain ones with homogeneous extension, or we may expect the child to learn to vary the extension of the compounds relevantly under variation of natural context. Moreover, in gauging his performance, we may ourselves be undecided as to which point he has gotten, with only limited sampling of his wielding of compounds.

Analogously, given a fragment containing the name "Linus," we may be unable to decide whether it refers to the child Linus of Argos or to Linus the son of Ismenius, whom Heracles killed with a lyre. But "refers" cannot here be taken as "denotes," for, in either case, nothing is denoted. The question, it seems, is rather what Linus-description may have denoted for the author of the fragment in question. Thus, in our finding "Linus" ambiguous, we are indirectly reflecting indecision as to the extension of "Linus-description" in this context.

Yet there is a residual problem in the case of replicas, which does not arise for nonreplicas. A "centaur" token differs in meaning from a "unicorn" token since a syntactically distinguishable group of "centaur" compounds diverges extensionally from another such group of "unicorn" compounds. The notion of *parallel* compounds implies that they are syntactically distinguishable and assignable to the two tokens differing in meaning. And the latter condition fails for *replicas* differing in meaning. Though extensional variation among compounds may occasion a kind of indecision respecting single tokens, disrupting learning or interpretation in the process, these varying compounds cannot be syntactically associated with the replicas that occasion the indecision in question; it is thus not clear what constitutes a resolution of the indecision.

Raymond, a given student of the novel, produces an "Algernon" token, which leaves us undecided as to how he would apply the compound "Algernon-description" – whether, in particular, he would thereby denote portions of Jones's novel or portions of Smith's. Deciding after a while in favor of Jones, we take Raymond's compound "Algernon-description" tokens to denote portions of Jones's novel. Yet, how does this decision respecting the compound affect the status of Raymond's original "Algernon" token? It remains as true now as before that it also occurs in all those compounds that denote portions of Smith's novel. Moreover, let us suppose that we have another student, George, who also produces an "Algernon" token and whose compound "Algernon-description" token denotes portions of Smith's rather than Jones's novel. Let us call Raymond's "Algernon" token A_1 and George's A_2; let us call Raymond's compound K_1 and George's K_2. K_1 and K_2 have, then, been decided to be extensionally divergent, but we want to say that this divergence of the compounds also flows inward, affecting the "meanings" of A_1 and A_2. We want, in short, to differentiate the latter on the basis of K_1 and K_2, but this is precisely what we cannot do, for A_1 occurs in *both* compounds, and so does A_2.

Since syntactic features are incapable of making the wanted distinctions, to associate A_1 with K_1 but not K_2, and A_2 with K_2 but not K_1 is, in effect, to presuppose a new notion of parallel compounds that cuts more finely than syntactic distinction will allow. We have seen that, where replicas are concerned, the very notion of parallel compounds, as originally conceived, *collapses* owing to the transitivity of the replica relation. What is needed then is appeal to some notion *other than* the replica relation.

We have already spoken of learning as providing some link between token and compound; the habits governing use of the token are associated with those governing use of the compounds. To wonder whether a given "Algernon" token is to be related to K_1 or K_2, it may now be suggested, is to wonder whether the habits governing the "Algernon" token in question are linked through learning with habits favoring K_1 or K_2. Can this account be made more specific? Can it, moreover, be freed from its dependence on the assumption of suitable compounds available to the producers of the original tokens? In the example of the "Linus" fragment discussed earlier, for instance, we imagined ourselves undecided as to whether the name referred to the child Linus of Argos or to Linus the son of Ismenius, and we characterized such indecision as concerning the denotation of "Linus-description" for the author of the fragment in question. But there may have been no such compound in the author's context and to talk, therefore, of linking his "Linus" habits with his "Linus-description" habits would thus be artificial.

A further consideration of the learning situation provides us with a clue. We noted that if a child withholds the term "centaur" from everything, we still do not judge him or her to have gotten the whole point until we are confident the child can correctly select centaur-pictures. Now in the selection of such pictures, the child does not, in fact, typically use the compound "centaur-picture," but rather the original term "centaur." We normally, moreover, ask the child to point out the centaur *in* a given picture, and he or she is expected to apply the same term "centaur" to some appropriate region of the picture. Such quasi-denotative uses of the term we shall call "mention-selective," for, though literally denoting neither centaur-pictures nor centaur-regions, it is here employed, in a manner reminiscent of metaphor, so as to select centaur-mentions in fact. In the case of "centaur," which has null (literal) denotation, its mention-selective employment seems clearly related to learning this denotation itself.

Mention-selective use is limited, however, neither to centaurs nor to children. A child is often asked to point out trees, dogs, and automobiles, for example, in picture books and magazines. And in our own typical labeling of a picture of a man "man" (rather than "man-picture"), we ourselves apply the term "man" to select not a man but a picture; we here apply the term not to what it denotes but rather to a mention thereof. Logicians have warned us so vehemently against confusing use with mention that we tend to overlook this employment of terms in actual learning and subsequent linguistic practice. The denotative and mention-selective uses are, it may be suggested, in fact intimately related, the one sometimes guiding the learning of the other and vice versa, the process resembling in significant ways the transfer phenomena characteristic of metaphor.

Consider the relation between the word "man" and man-pictures; the word is used not only to select men but to sort pictures of men. "Man" literally denotes men and "man-picture" literally denotes man-pictures, but "man" is also transferred and applied mention-selectively to man-pictures. If a person has mastered the conventional use of the term "man," he or she is normally expected to employ it properly not only in pointing out men but also in selecting man-pictures, and man-regions within such pictures. The habits governing the person's employment of "man" tokens in application to men are supposed, that is, to guide (and perhaps be guided by) his or her application of such tokens to man-mentions.[25]

Returning now to Raymond and George, the difference in meaning of their respective "Algernon" tokens does not lie in their primary extensions but rather in their mention-selective applications. That is to say, A_1 mention-selects the extension of K_1;

---

25 In *Languages of Art*, Goodman stresses that labels or descriptions are themselves sorted by other labels, as well as effecting a sorting of elements themselves, the labeling of labels being independent of what these latter are labels for. "Objects are classified under 'desk'. . . . Descriptions are classified under 'desk-description'" (p. 31). What is being suggested at present is that the labeling of labels may be effected not by a new compound but by a habit-guided transfer of the original label itself. (See also *Languages of Art*, Part II, sec. 5–8, for treatments of metaphor and transfer.) Reverse transfers, we suggest, may also take place.

48

and A_2 mention-selects the extension of K_2. Given a portion of Jones's novel or a suitable portrait of its hero, we ask whether Raymond or George would be prepared to apply an "Algernon" token to it by way of mention-selective transfer. Our indecision with respect to the "Linus" fragment is, similarly, an indecision as to what descriptions or pictures or other portrayals are mention-selected by its constituent "Linus" token. We ask, in effect, what mentions the author's habits led him, or would have led him, to point out by using this token or suitable replicas thereof. This is also analogous for our indivisible "greencentaur" tokens; though lacking elementary ambiguity, they may vary in what they mention-select.

Derivative compound ambiguity, initially introduced as consisting in elementary ambiguity of secondary extension (i.e., of compounds), is thus reformulated as variation in mention-selection characterizing the original tokens themselves. Replicas, it is suggested, may vary in mention-selection despite their syntactical indistinguishability; we may estimate one, but not another, to be linked through mention-selection with some particular extension of an ambiguous compound of our construction. One noncompound replica may then, indeed, differ in meaning from another with the same primary extension, through differing in its mention-selection. If it be said that the concept of derivative compound ambiguity still depends on the notion of extensionally divergent *compounds* for its *explanation,* it is nevertheless not presupposed that either the concept or its explanation is shared by producers of the replicas we are concerned to interpret. We may judge by means of compounds available to us; we need not also attribute knowledge or employment of these compounds to the users whose replicas are in question. Yet we may conclude that the extensional divergence represented by such compounds flows inward to differentiate the meanings of constituent replicas.[26]

26 In my *Beyond the Letter* (London: Routledge, 1979), pp. 17–20, this treatment of ambiguity is supplemented by an analysis of multiple meaning, where a token is to be interpreted as holding two or more rival extensions.

Chapter 4

Ambiguity in pictures

Ambiguity pertains not only to language but also to pictures. Pictorial ambiguity presents independent problems of interpretation, however, since the notion of replication, that is, sameness of spelling – which is useful in explicating linguistic ambiguity – is not applicable to pictures.[1] Yet pictures often involve the sort of ambivalence associated with ambiguous expressions, and pictures are indeed frequently described as ambiguous. How, then, is pictorial ambiguity to be understood? That is our present problem.

1 WHAT AMBIGUITY IS NOT

The problem needs refinement, for ordinary attributions of ambiguity to pictures are too elastic to be of theoretical interest. A picture that represents something unfamiliar, improbable, fantastic, or impossible may surprise or take one aback but need not be ambiguous, strictly speaking, any more than a corresponding representation in words. Nor are mere generality or vagueness to be confused with ambiguity. A picture of a woodpecker in Peterson's *Field Guide to the Birds East of the Rockies* makes a general

"Ambiguity in Pictures" appeared as "Pictorial Ambiguity," *Journal of Aesthetics and Art Criticism*, 47, no. 2 (Spring 1989), 109–15.

1 See Chapter 3. The inapplicability of replication to pictures is argued in Nelson Goodman, *Languages of Art* (Indianapolis, Ind.: Hackett, 1976), p. 115.

reference to woodpeckers but is not therefore ambiguous.[2] Nor is a picture of a finch ambiguous in leaving one undecided as to whether the bird at the feeder is a finch or not.

Everyday uses of the term "ambiguous" typically override such niceties, whether in regard to pictures or words. It is well known that linguistic ambiguity is often confused with vagueness or generality in ordinary parlance. And while descriptions of physically impossible states, for example, "water flowing uphill", are hardly considered ambiguous, pictures of such states often are, as witnessed by M. C. Escher's lithograph *Waterfall,* in which water is depicted as falling from a height to turn a waterwheel, thence flowing back upward to its initial height.[3] That no watercourse answers to such a picture does not imply that there is some indecision between one denotation and another. A picture of a mermaid, which, like the phrase "half woman half fish", denotes nothing, is no more ambiguous than the phrase.

It might be protested that there is a conflict of expectations engendered by the mermaid-picture, each half arousing expectations violated by the other, but there is in such conflict as yet no germ of ambiguity. The picture may be perfectly clear in its mode of depiction, and it is indeed clear enough to be judged as denotatively null. Similarly, any statement of the form "*p* and not *p*" might be said to engender conflicting expectations, each half violating the expectations aroused by the other. Yet the statement is not on this account ambiguous; it is in fact clear enough to be clearly false.

2 AMBIGUITY AND INDECISION

Elementary ambiguity (E-ambiguity) consists in extensional variation across replicas, each of which may, however, be perfectly definite in its application. Thus, for example, two "now" inscriptions produced at different times are replica related yet extensionally divergent, hence E-ambiguous with respect to one an-

2 Roger Tory Peterson, *A Field Guide to the Birds East of the Rockies* (Boston: Houghton Mifflin, 1980), pp. 191, 193, 263.
3 M. C. Escher and J. L. Lochner, *The World of M. C. Escher* (New York: Abrams, 1971), p. 147.

other, neither presenting any interpretive problem.[4] Derivatively, each "now" may be deemed E-ambiguous (categorically) in being E-ambiguous with respect to the other – though neither occasions any indecision. By contrast, however, indecision may indeed affect a single token, caught between rival readings, each vying to be chosen as its sole interpretation. Here we have I-ambiguity, which involves an interpretive ambivalence or indecision, rather than a mere conflict of expectations between parts.[5]

Now E-ambiguity is clearly inapplicable to pictures, since pictures have no spelling system and thus are not replica related. But we might think it feasible to extend the notion of I-ambiguity to pictures that are indeed subject to rival interpretations. That the parts of a picture engender conflicting expectations implies no such ambivalence or indecision affecting either it or its parts; indeed, such internal conflict may itself resolve the interpretation of the whole, as we have seen. In cases of I-ambiguity, however, the description or picture remains suspended between conflicting interpretations, each of which makes maximally good sense of it in context.

It should be added, in passing, that our present problem concerns pictures specifically, that is, representations operating under interpretive presumptions, no matter how informal or tacit. Such conventions serve to rule out certain interpretations as wrong, even if, as in I-ambiguous cases, they allow rival interpretations to survive. Rorschach inkblots, although they indeed evoke different descriptions from subjects required to interpret them, are hardly on that account to be reckoned as pictorially ambiguous, since no proffered interpretation is precluded. The inkblots, in functioning as diagnostic instruments, are hospitable to any and all interpretations placed upon them.

Now to extend the *general notion* of I-ambiguity (i.e., interpretive rivalry) from language to pictures is one thing; to extend the *analysis* of that notion as well is quite another. For I-ambiguity involves E-ambiguity, the indecision over the token flowing from

4 See Chapter 3. Also Scheffler, *Beyond the Letter* (London: Routledge, 1979), pp. 12–15.
5 Ibid., pp. 15–16.

its type variability, that is, from extensional variation among its replicas. Thus, for an I-ambiguous token x with two rival interpretations, each interpretation takes x as coextensive with one or another of its divergent replicas z and y, respectively. Such an account is, however, again unavailable for an ambiguous picture, since it has no replicas, divergent or otherwise.

Nevertheless, perhaps an extension of the analysis in question might be made to apply, that is, some looser relation than replication might serve to connect the ambiguous picture to mutually divergent others. The operative conventions of picturing, whatever they may be, are after all general in scope. They thus relate the picture to others one has seen. Moreover, in combination with contextual clues, they may be expected, on occasion, to support conflicting interpretations of the very same picture.

Such conventions of picturing, for example, will guide you in reading my rough street map, but I may have left it unclear whether the circle indicating where you are to turn refers to the stop light or the blinking yellow – although clearly it must be the one or the other, comparable maps I have on other occasions provided you having employed the circle sometimes for red lights alone, sometimes also for yellows. The outline of a human form in a picture may represent a person or rather a shadow cast on a wall; the picture may be interpreted equally well either way under the interpretive conventions taken as operative in context.

As distinct from *vagueness* of a word-inscription x, involving mere indecision as to its applicability in certain cases, the *ambiguity* of x typically requires in addition that maximally satisfactory though conflicting resolutions of such indecision be available, each associated with divergent replicas z and y. Similarly, mere indecision as to a picture's applicability does not yet imply its ambiguity, but only one or another sort of vagueness. For the picture to be, in addition, ambiguous, we need maximally satisfactory, though conflicting, resolutions of the indecision, each one relatable to other pictures than the one in question.

Often, the viewer will oscillate between such conflicting interpretations, trying now this one, now that, in the attempt to fix upon one. Where, indeed, one interpretation alone is the correct one, the indecision in question may be resolved, on occasion, by broadening the initial context, importing fresh information. Cases of this sort are thus similar to I-ambiguity in the case of language, where the conflict of interpretations is resolvable only by choosing between them. Later on, I will discuss multiple meaning (M-ambiguity), where the problem is rather how simultaneously to accommodate, rather than to choose between, rival interpretations.[6] But first a new problem needs to be faced.

3 BEYOND EXTENSIONS: CAPTION AND ILLUSTRATION

The ambiguity of a picture has so far been discussed in terms of the availability of conflicting interpretations, understood extensionally. But pictures may be ambiguous even when the conflicting interpretations in question are coextensive. If a picture is either of a centaur or of a unicorn in the distance, the indecision between these rival interpretations can hardly be understood extensionally, for the picture under either interpretation denotes nothing.

It is conceivable that, in some such cases, the ambiguity might be pinned on a *part* of the picture, itself undecided as between differing extensions. Thus, in our preceding example, it might be that the critical portion of the picture is undecidable as between its denoting an animal horn or an animal ear. Such cases would parallel compound predicate tokens with I-ambiguous constituents where it is the extension of these *constituents* rather than of the compounds themselves that is at stake.[7] Thus, for example, a given "green centaur" token, as a whole extensionally null, contains a constituent "green" token that might be subject to rival extensional readings, that is, as denoting certain colored things or, rather, as denoting inexperienced things. Extending this general idea to pictures, we could then take pictorial ambiguity to include cases in which picture parts were extensionally undecidable, even where the extension of the whole was unaffected. However, it is too much to expect that every instance of the sort that concerns us

6 Ibid., pp. 17–20.
7 Ibid., p. 29.

will in fact have such undecidable parts. We must, therefore, seek an account of pictorial ambiguity that does not depend on conflicting extensions, whether of the whole or of its parts.

It is worth remarking that the problem does not hinge on null extensions but rather on coextensiveness, of which the preceding example of the null picture affords a convenient illustration. Consider further the Necker cube – strictly, the Necker-cube-picture – widely considered to be ambiguous.[8] This picture, presumably of a transparent cube, can be taken to depict the cube as seen from above or as seen from below. In either case, the picture may be understood to denote (transparent) cubes in general, and assuming such an understanding, the rival interpretations are clearly coextensive. Nor is it readily apparent how to pin the presumed ambiguity on any part. The denotation thus is constant, while the interpetation varies. Under one interpretation, the picture denotes cubes and is a cube-seen-from-above-picture, whereas, under the other interpetation, it denotes cubes but is rather a cube-seen-from-below-picture. What oscillates here is not the denotation of the picture but our characterization of it, not its extension but rather its type.

Each such characterization in effect relates the picture in question to others, and the pictures with which one characterization classifies it are, in general, different from those with which the other classifies it. The fundamental point, however, is that we have here another source of ambiguity than the picture's extension or denotation. We are dealing in these cases with its type, that is to say, with its *description or characterization,* or alternatively, with the *mode of its captioning.* To say that we cannot decide whether to call something a "unicorn-picture" or a "centaur-picture" is to put the matter in terms of description or characterization; the question here is not what the picture denotes, but rather whether it is itself denoted or characterized by one or another of these compound predicates. To say that we cannot decide

8 W. N. Dember, *Visual Perception: The Nineteenth Century* (New York: Wiley, 1964), pp. 76–80, including excerpts from the last two pages of L. A. Necker's letter to the editor of *Philosophical Magazine* ("On an optical phenomenon which occurs on viewing a figure of a crystal or geometrical solid," 3rd series [1832], 329–37).

whether to label the picture "unicorn" or "centaur" is to refer rather to its mode of captioning, for these latter labels, though fitting as captions, denote nothing. They *mention-select* the pictures or other symbols to which they are appropriate as captions.[9] Similarly, "cube seen from below" and "cube seen from above" may serve as rival captions for the cube-picture, between which we may vacillate. But (unlike "cube-seen-from-below-picture" and "cube-seen-from-above-picture") they do not *denote* the picture, which is not a cube.

There is an advantage to putting the matter in terms of captioning or, more generally, in terms of *mention-selection* rather than in terms of *characterization*. For ambiguity is a property of symbols affecting their reference, that is, their manner of referring. There is thus something odd in considering a picture ambiguous not on account of its own reference but on account of the reference of *other* symbols to it. To be said to belong to the denotation of a term, for example, "unicorn-picture," is not something that characterizes the picture's own referring. The case of mention-selection is different, however. For if a symbol x mention-selects another y, then the converse is also true. Thus, to say that a symbol (e.g., a cube-picture) is mention-selected by certain others (e.g., a "cube seen from above" and a "cube seen from below") tells us something about the symbol's (i.e., the cube-picture's) own referential functioning.

Mention-selection is quite general as a relation among symbols of various sorts. The term "man" mention-selects not only man-pictures but also man-descriptions, for example, "man"; and man-pictures mention-select man-descriptions as well as other man-pictures. Thus, the term "mention-selection" is broader than the colloquial term "caption," introduced earlier, since a word may caption a picture, but a picture may not caption a word. If we seek a narrower term to serve as the converse of "caption," we may use "illustration," each of these being a subrelation of mention-selection. Thus, a picture mention-selected by a caption illustrates it. A diagram of a pump in a dictionary or encyclopedia

9 See Chapter 3; also Scheffler, *Beyond the Letter*, pp. 31-6.

mention-selects, and is mention-selected by, the entry word "pump"; is captioned by it; and in turn illustrates it. We must be careful not to confuse *illustration,* as thus characterized, with *satisfaction* or with *exemplification,* in Goodman's terminology. The pump-diagram, not being a pump, does not satisfy the predicate "pump" but only illustrates it. Nor, a fortiori, does the diagram exemplify "pump," not only satisfying, but also referring to it.[10]

The indecision as to whether "unicorn" or "centaur" captions the picture means, then, that there is an indecision as to whether the picture illustrates "unicorn" or "centaur." This ambiguity affecting the picture's reference relates not to what it denotes, of course, but rather to what it illustrates or, more generally, to what it mention-selects. The indecision over the caption is thus one with the indecision over the picture; it cuts both ways.

Something similar may be said about vagueness. If I cannot decide whether to caption a picture of a catlike creature with feathers "cat" or not, equally I cannot decide whether the picture illustrates "cat" or not. The vagueness is mutual and does not reside in the caption alone. The indecision here is whether to link the caption ("cat") with the picture or not – to apply or to withhold it – as contrasted with the cases of ambiguity we have been discussing, where the indecision is rather whether to apply one ("unicorn") rather than another ("centaur") caption to the picture. However, whether the indecision is one of vagueness or one of ambiguity, it affects not only caption but picture as well.

4 MULTIPLE MEANING

We have been discussing cases of indecision presuming that one interpretation alone is the correct one. But the Necker-cube-picture is hard to treat that way. It seems to bear both rival inter-

10 Goodman, *Languages of Art,* pp. 52–7. Of course, the diagram satisfies the predicate "pump-diagram," but whether it also exemplifies it depends on whether, as seems unlikely, the diagram *refers* to this predicate, i.e., to the property of being a pump-diagram. There may, however, indeed be cases of genuine exemplificational ambiguity, where we are undecided as between different predicates exemplified by a given picture or other symbol.

pretations. The duck–rabbit figure is similar in this respect.[11] The oscillation between rival interpretations in these cases is permanent, that is, the rivalry is not to be resolved in favor of one or the other, but rather to be domesticated – taken as part of the function of the symbol in question. The ambiguity here involves simultaneous multiplicity of meanings rather than indecision between one meaning and another.

The duck–rabbit picture (D–R) is neither a duck-and-rabbit-picture nor a duck-or-rabbit-picture. Unlike the former, it cannot be analyzed as containing a duck-picture part and a rabbit-picture part. And unlike the latter, it does not blandly welcome every duck and rabbit into its reference rather than accepting only ducks or only rabbits. It oscillates – now appearing to accept ducks while excluding rabbits, now the reverse. For each duck and for each rabbit, it says yes and also no.

It is not that the D–R is either a duck-picture or a rabbit-picture but we cannot decide which. It is rather that we are tempted to say it is both a duck-picture (as a whole), denoting all and only ducks, and also a rabbit-picture (as a whole), denoting all and only rabbits, all the while knowing full well that it is neither, and that to consider it to be both is, moreover, self-contradictory.

Now the presumption of a simultaneous multiplicity of meanings might be questioned, as follows: Since one cannot see the D–R as both a duck-picture *and* a rabbit-picture at the same time, it is an oscillation between meanings rather than a simultaneous multiplicity that we have to deal with here; such oscillation may, moreover, be treated by time slicing, that is, by distinguishing the references of temporal parts of the picture. It is thus, for example, that the apparent ambiguity of a portable "No Parking Here" sign may be resolved, assigning different references to each time slice with a different location.[12]

There are, however, various reasons militating against such a course in the present instance. In the first place, if we were to take

11 See L. Wittgenstein, *Philosophical Investigations* (Oxford: Basil Blackwell, 1953), p. 194; Wittgenstein credits J. Jastrow's *Fact and Fable in Psychology* (Freeport, N.Y.: Books for Libraries Press, reprint of 1901 Edition, 1971) for the figure.
12 See Nelson Goodman, *The Structure of Appearance*, 3rd ed. (Dordrecht: D. Reidel, 1977), p. 264.

the facts of perceptual oscillation as decisive in the question before us, time slicing itself would prove inadequate. For, unlike the "No Parking Here" sign, the reference of which changes with each change of location but is constant for each location across observers, the D–R would carry conflicting references at each moment for which different observers were seeing it differently. The reference would need to be relativized not only to time but also to observer, thus making for a complexity that would be unmanageable.

Second, the perceptual oscillation of the D–R is part of its functioning in a way that differs from the changing reference of the "No Parking Here" sign. The sign works perfectly well even if never moved, and I may understand its function perfectly well in such a case. But if I never saw the D–R as a duck-picture but only as a rabbit-picture, I would be missing a crucial point about its functioning.

Third, the D–R is, in this respect, much like a written pun, the conflicting interpretations of which may oscillate in the mind and do so differently for different readers. Here, we do not say each time slice of the pun carries one or another meaning for each reader at the precise time the meaning in question is entertained by each. Rather, we abstract from the varying histories of readers who see now one point, now another, and take the enduring pun as carrying its conflicting meanings simultaneously. The point can be generalized to include not only puns but texts construed as enduring works with multiple and conflicting interpretations. The D–R is thus taken here as conveying two conflicting meanings simultaneously, the point being not to choose one of these as alone correct, but rather to grasp and preserve both.

Now, puns are M-ambiguous, providing clear examples of the general phenomenon of multiple meaning.[13] The challenge of the M-ambiguous token is that it threatens us with inconsistency. If a token x within a sentence frame F is presumed to have two different extensions, some object belongs to one but not the other of those extensions, and is therefore both denoted and not denoted by x. We may, however, interpret the token x as having

13 Scheffler, *Beyond the Letter*, pp. 17–20.

no extension of its own, thus obviating the threat of inconsistency; however, since it replicates extensionally divergent tokens z and y, which, combined respectively with x's frame F, produce two different potential sentences, it manages to convey the double meaning in question. This strategy cannot, however, be extended to the interpretation of the D–R, insofar as it depends on replication, which is not available for pictures as it is for languages.

But perhaps, it might be suggested, a looser relation than replication may serve to similar effect here, as in the case discussed earlier of a picture interpretable in different ways under operative conventions of picturing. We could then say, for example, that the right half of the D–R is related to other pictures one has seen of rabbit's ears and equally related to others one has seen of duck's beaks. The D–R's right half might then be taken as having no extension of its own, but rather as conveying two meanings by its relatedness, as thus described, to pictures with divergent extension.

The difficulty with this idea is that the required notion of potential picture could not be applied analogously to that of potential sentence. For, unlike the potential sentence, where z need only be a replica of x in order to combine with x's frame F to form such a sentence – all else being irrelevant and, therefore, only a wrong relative location precluding actual sentencehood – the same cannot be said of the rabbit's-ear-picture loosely related to the D–R. It would, for example, need additionally to be of appropriate size and shape to form a picture in combination with the left half of the D–R. The interpretation of the D–R cannot well be made to depend on the availability of such exactly appropriate related pictures.

The idea of completability may be suggested as offering a more promising interpretation. For whether taken as a duck-picture or a rabbit-picture, the D–R is a picture of an animal's head, without the body. It is thus completable in alternative ways, so as to form either a duck-picture or a rabbit-picture. Suppose, then, we take the D–R, supplemented by an appropriately shaped lower region, to constitute a potential duck-picture while taking the D–R, supplemented by another such region, to constitute a potential rabbit-picture. We then interpret the D–R's multiple meaning thus: As part of a potential duck-picture, it denotes a duck's head, while as part of a potential rabbit-picture, it denotes a rabbit's head.

The fatal flaw in this idea is that completability yields multiple meaning wherever we look. Any single short straight line turns out M-ambiguous, since it is the common part of indefinitely many divergent potential pictures. The D–R is, moreover, completable in innumerably many ways so as to yield pictures quite different from duck-pictures and rabbit-pictures. Finally, the Necker-cube-picture is not incomplete in the same way as the D–R and cannot, even putatively, be interpreted along the lines of this suggestion.

These difficulties point to the need for a new direction. Perhaps the trouble is that we have been following the lead of language too closely. Specifically, we have taken the pun as our example and sought to locate different bearers of the rival denotations that seem to be involved. Taking a cue from the preceding section, we shall now interpret multiple meaning in terms of mention-selection rather than of denotation, the two notions being more loosely related than we might initially have supposed.

Thus, I said earlier that we are tempted to say of the D–R that it is both a duck-picture, denoting all and only ducks, and also a rabbit-picture, denoting all and only rabbits, all the while knowing that to consider it to be both is self-contradictory. Of course, since no duck is a rabbit, to say that the D–R denotes ducks and ducks alone is inconsistent with its denoting rabbits and rabbits only. But – and here is the critical point – to say that something is a duck-picture is to characterize its type; this characterization does not imply that the D–R denotes all and only ducks. Goodman has, for example, discussed the case of an infant-picture representing, that is, denoting, Churchill, as well as that of a picture denoting a horse while failing to be a horse-picture, since representing the horse as a light speck in the distance.[14]

Once the link with denotation is broken, there is no longer any inconsistency in supposing the D–R to be both a duck-picture and a rabbit-picture. Put in terms of mention-selection, we may say

14 Goodman, *Languages of Art*, pp. 29–30.

that both "duck" and "rabbit" (but not "duck and rabbit") are suitable captions for the picture, which illustrates them both, the picture and each caption mention-selecting one another, although, of course, neither caption mention-selects the other one. As for denotation, it may be decided independently for each D–R: We may decide, for example, that it has no denotation, or denotes both ducks and rabbits, or has still another extension in context. The special character of the D–R is that whereas most duck-pictures and rabbit-pictures take one or the other caption exclusively, it takes both; and each caption, moreover, diverges extensionally, as well as differing in its mention-selective range, from the other.

The Necker-cube-picture may be treated similarly, "cube seen from below" and "cube seen from above" each serving as an appropriate caption for the figure, while diverging extensionally from the other. There is no indecision here between rival denotations (as earlier noted), but rather an appropriateness of divergent captions for the picture.

M-ambiguity, thus understood in terms of mention-selection, goes beyond the extensional interpretation of puns discussed earlier. The notion of *multiple meaning*, in which divergent captions are simultaneously mention-selected by a given symbol, offers one general way of understanding how a single work may, at one and the same time, bear conflicting interpretations.[15]

I speculate that at least part of the fascination of M-ambiguous works derives from the suspicion of inconsistency, the fear (or perhaps the hope) that logic has been breached. I have suggested that a confusion of denotation with mention-selection underlies a variety of phenomena described by psychologists and anthropologists, for example, attribution of causal powers to words, word magic, and so on.[16] Perhaps the same deep-rooted confusion gives rise to the feeling that terms with discrete denotations cannot, in logic, mention-select the same symbols, that a picture,

---

15 See, in this connection, Nelson Goodman and Catherine Z. Elgin, "Interpretation and Identity: Can the Work Survive the World"? *Critical Inquiry*, 12 (1986), 564–75, esp. 573.
16 See Section I, this volume.

for example, cannot at once illustrate divergent captions. When, nevertheless, a picture does seem to do so, logic totters, with fascination the result.

A final word should be added here concerning the phenomenon of pictorial metaphor. Since metaphor in language is a species of ambiguity, a metaphorical token being interpreted in the light of an earlier ambiguous replica, pictorial metaphor clearly requires a different treatment. We cannot simply transfer the linguistic analysis to the pictorial case, since, as we have seen, the notion of a replica is here unavailable. Yet what is presumed in instances of pictorial metaphor is that the picture in question can be "read" literally as well as metaphorically. How shall we interpret this situation?

Here is a picture of a skull, the picture metaphorically referring to death. The picture is literally a skull-picture but only metaphorically a death-picture. In effect, it takes the caption "skull" literally, illustrating "skull" literally but illustrating "death" only metaphorically, "skull" itself being a metaphor for death. And this description can, in turn, be understood as follows: The picture takes both captions, "skull" and "death," simultaneously, being M-ambiguous, with one caption distinguishable as literal relative to the other.

Section III
Symbol and metaphor

Chapter 5

Ten myths of metaphor

Various myths surround the topic of metaphor. I here criticize 10 such myths, hoping thereby to open the way to a better understanding of the topic.

1 THE MYTH OF FALSEHOOD

Only literal statements are true, according to this myth. All the rest distort and falsify. The poets (as Plato taught us) lie; only the scientists tell the truth. To describe an unreliable, cowardly, or sickly person as a weak reed is just to speak a falsehood, which becomes a truth through negation: obviously, the person referred to is *not* a weak reed.

But it is *obvious* that he is not a weak reed only if "weak reed" is taken *literally,* for it is, indeed, obvious that no person is literally a reed, weak or otherwise. And it is utterly trivial to say that a metaphorical statement, *taken literally,* may be false. Taken metaphorically, however, the statement may well be true: He is indeed a weak reed, and it is false to deny that he is. To be sure, metaphorical assertions are eligible for falsehood. But they are, no more than literal assertions, always false.[1]

"Ten Myths of Metaphor" appeared in *Journal of Aesthetic Education,* 22, no. 1 (Spring 1988), 45–50.

1 Donald Davidson, "What Metaphors Mean," *Critical Inquiry,* 5, no. 1 (1978), 32, claims that "a metaphor doesn't say anything beyond its literal meaning (nor

2 THE MYTH OF EMBELLISHMENT

If not always false, then metaphors are always, at any rate, cognitively contentless; so runs the present myth. Rhetorical adornments merely, metaphors can (and, for the sake of theoretical clarity, should) always be stripped away, allowing the bare literal truth to shine forth.

But what remains after the metaphor is removed from the statement "War is hell"? Eliminating the predicate leaves a bare grammatical subject, not even a full sentence, true or false. Presumably, what is intended here is not mere removal but translation, or replacement by a cognitive equivalent. It is, notoriously, no easy task to specify criteria for such replacement. But the more fundamental point is this: To concede that the metaphorical attribution *has* a cognitive equivalent is to admit that it possesses cognitive content, after all. It is, of course, not in any case true that metaphors with cognitive content always have literal equivalents.

3 THE MYTH OF EMOTIVITY

Metaphors are, according to this myth, emotive and not at all, or not primarily, cognitive. Whatever may be said of cognitive equivalents, metaphors surely have no emotive equivalents. It is their high emotivity that sets them apart from literal statements, making them irreplaceable.

But is "a sparkling intelligence" or "a pedestrian analysis" highly emotive? Is, indeed, the doctor's metaphorical "You face an uphill struggle for your life" more emotive than "The tests show that you have cancer"? Whatever criteria may be specified for the elusive property of emotivity, literal expressions, too, may have it in abundance, as witness "neutron bomb," "Chernobyl," and "leukemia." Emotions develop in the most intimate connection with cognitions; feelings respond to things as apprehended and comprehended. Why should literal accounts of things be any

does its maker say anything, in using the metaphor, beyond the literal)." His view has been amply, and to my mind decisively, criticized by Max Black, "How Metaphors Work: A Reply to Donald Davidson," *Critical Theory*, 6, no. 1 (1979), 131–43, and Nelson Goodman, *Critical Theory*, 6, no. 1 (1979), 125–30.

less related to the emotive life than metaphorical accounts? Why should emotional response to things cognized be better expressed by metaphorical than literal reference to such things?[2]

4 THE MYTH OF SUGGESTIVENESS

Metaphorical statements are false or contentless, but at least they are distinctive in their suggestiveness, according to the present myth. Cognitively deficient themselves, they nevertheless stimulate associations of ideas that may terminate in useful truths.

Why literal statements are thought to be poorer than metaphorical ones in their suggestive capabilities is not explained by this myth. Associations of ideas, after all, occur in response to all sorts of verbal (let alone nonverbal) stimulation. They are even set off by pure nonsense, for example, in "Jabberwocky"; why are literal statements, in particular, deficient?

What this myth overlooks is that metaphorical statements that initiate new classifications and categories do so not, as nonsense syllables stimulate, by adventitious means, but through their own novel assertive content. They may indeed begin as metaphorical hypotheses, but they often (and without change of content) end as acknowledged truths, their once startling attributions now congealed into new literal references. That the table is a swarm of atoms, that we live at the bottom of a sea of air, that the mind processes information or forms images – these are by now literal cliches, the same statements having started life as bold metaphors.[3]

5 THE MYTH OF COMMUNICATION

Such examples refute the myth of metaphors as exclusively devices of communication. This myth supposes that the thought

---

2 On emotive views of metaphor, see my *Beyond the Letter* (London: Routledge, 1979), pp. 87–92.
3 See Willird Van Orman Quine, "A Postscript on Metaphor," *Critical Theory*, 5, no. 1 (1978), 161–2, for examples of metaphors "serving us at the growing edge of science" and then turning literal with apt use, in application to the same referents.

is fully available to the thinker in purely literal terms, but that its communication requires, or is facilitated by, the use of metaphors. Metaphor is the packaging of literal thoughts for transmission to others, but forms no part of these thoughts themselves.

What is thus denied is the patent fact that metaphor serves the seeker and not alone the transmitter of truth, that scientific theorizing, for example, thrives on metaphorical description put forth in an investigative spirit. The theorist typically does not know in advance the detailed basis of the metaphorical description he or she proposes, guessing that a certain deliberate crossing of categories may be found increasingly significant with further inquiry. The metaphor embodying this guess does not require a prior determination of such significance. On the contrary, the metaphorical description itself serves as an *invitation*, to its originator and to others, to develop its ramifications. Its challenge is not to receive a fully substantiated message, but to find or invent new and fruitful descriptions of nature.

6 THE MYTH OF OWNERSHIP

The present myth supposes that the author of a metaphor has exclusive rights or privileged access to it. As an instrumental device of communication, it is wholly under the control of its creator, shaped exclusively by his or her intent. Interpretation of a metaphor requires, ultimately, appeal to such intent.

What is here left out of the account, as already noted in the past section, is the exploratory or heuristic role of metaphor. What this role implies, in particular, is that the author of a metaphor has no special key to its import, no privileged access, no rights of ownership. In creating a metaphor, one may surprise oneself. The invitation presented by a metaphorical utterance may lead us to rethink old material in the light of new categorizations or to consider newly discovered phenomena in terms already available. Whether the task be to incorporate the novel or to reorganize the familiar, metaphor serves often as a probe for connections that may improve understanding or spark theoretical advance.

7 THE MYTH OF METAPHORICAL TRUTH

This myth holds that there are two species of truth, the one literal, the other metaphorical. "The match flamed" is held to be true in a way quite different from that in which "His eyes flamed" may be true. Adherents of this myth are thus seduced into a fruitless hunt for the special characteristics of metaphorical as distinct from literal truth, yearning for an essential difference between poetic and scientific utterance.

That the two sentences differ may be readily admitted. But that their difference is to be located in the duality of truth is dubious. For each sentence is true under the selfsame general condition: ". . ." is true if and only if . . . . Thus, "The match flamed" is true if and only if the match flamed, and "His eyes flamed" is true if and only if his eyes indeed flamed. That the first "flamed" differs in its extension from the second is a fact about these two replicas in particular, not a fact about what it means for their respective sentences to be true. Nor, a fortiori, does it require the postulation of two species of truth.

8 THE MYTH OF CONSTANCY

This myth holds that once a metaphor, always a metaphor. Contrary to the view that the literal is primary while the metaphorical is mere embellishment, the present myth declares the metaphorical to be primary, since every term in use has indeed a metaphorical lineage. All speech is thus declared metaphorical.

A consequence of this myth is that the notion of the literal is emptied of content; correlatively, the notion of metaphor, as contrasting category, loses its point. This consequence is, however, avoidable, and without denying the pervasiveness of metaphorical lineage: What needs only to be acknowledged is the historical dimension – the fact that the literal-metaphorical contrast is effective not absolutely, but relative to time.

Given two extensionally divergent replicas of a term, that is, two tokens of a certain type at a given time, we deem the one metaphorical whose interpretation is typically, or optimally, guided by an understanding of the other, which we take as literal.

A coextensive replica of this metaphorical expression occurring *at a later time* may quite properly, however, be judged to be literal. The term, construed as the type, has altered in its metaphorical status over time. The first description of an electronic device as a *calculator* was metaphorical; nowadays such a description is literal.

9 THE MYTH OF FORMULA

How nice it would be to have a simple formula for decoding metaphorical expressions. The myth that there is such a formula is an old one, often criticized but never eliminated. Indeed, it is likely to gain a new life with the aid of current computer technology and associated models of the mind.

The fact is that metaphorical expressions are not coded. They have no recipes, nor can they be exhaustively enumerated in dictionaries or codebooks. Understanding a metaphor requires interpretation and investigation in context.

The most popular candidate for a formula to shortcut such interpretation and investigation is the concept of similarity. It is, however, a vacuous concept, there being too many similarities to choose from. Similarities abound wherever one looks, but few will support true metaphorical descriptions. On the other hand, to supplement the notion of similarity with that of importance (i.e., to seek important similarities) introduces an ineradicable contextual reference, which cannot itself be compressed into a formula. Here inspection of the context, ingenuity, and wit are required to take up the slack. In place of an automatic readout from a codebook or the routine application of a formula, we have an interpretive process of search and discovery.

10 THE MYTH OF OBJECTUALISM

Comparison of objects, as suggested in the foregoing references to similarity, is certainly involved in metaphorical description, but it is a myth to suppose that only comparison of objects is involved. According to this myth, one compares the objects denoted metaphorically by a term with those denoted literally by that term. For

example, in "Men are wolves," "wolves" is metaphorically applied to men, while literally denoting members of *Canis lupus*. Abstracting the features common to both sets of objects, one interprets the metaphor as attributing certain of these features, for example, fierceness, to the metaphorical referent.

This myth is misguided not only because comparison and abstraction are too broad, requiring restriction by what wants attention in context. The further point is that metaphor is not wholly objectual in outlook. Its routes of comparison are often circuitous, touching not only on the objects in question and their features, but also on various representations of these objects. That wolves are, it is said, rather more pacific than their familiar stereotype will allow does not disqualify "Men are wolves" as a metaphorical attribution of fierceness to men. It is the stereotype representing wolves rather than features of the wolves themselves that gives the clue to this attribution. Nor does "The boss is a dragon" lack all sense in consequence of the fact that "dragon" has no objects at all to denote. Again, representative stereotypes (in this case, dragon images, descriptions, models, and portrayals) come to the rescue. For the term "dragon" serves not only as a denoting unit that in fact denotes nothing, but also as a caption for dragon-mentions, which are in fact, as indicated, plentiful. Such mention-selection aids the understanding of metaphors. We live, after all, in a world of symbols as well as other objects. Our view of objects and our knowledge of their representations serve alike as resources for interpretation.

Chapter 6
Metaphor and context

In his *Languages of Art,* Goodman proposes a general approach to metaphor that emphasizes its contextual character. I will here review the basic features of his treatment and then offer some critical comments in defense of a revised version of contextualism. I begin, then, with an account of Goodman's views.

1 CONTEXTUALISM AND METAPHOR

Metaphor, says Goodman, "is a matter of teaching an old word new tricks – of applying an old label in a new way."[1] This characterization is, however, not sufficient, since "every application of a predicate to a new event or a newfound object is new; but such routine projection does not constitute metaphor." The further characterization offered is as follows:

"Metaphor and Context" is drawn from *Beyond the Letter,* Part III, Sections 9, 10, 11.
1 Nelson Goodman, *Languages of Art,* 2nd ed. (Indianapolis, Ind.: Hackett, 1986), p. 69. (Goodman does not himself describe his treatment as contextual: Contextualism is an interpretation that I suggest fits his treatment.) My discussion of metaphor in *Beyond the Letter* (London: Routledge, 1979) offers critical accounts also of intuitionistic, emotivist, formulaic, intensionalistic, and interactional approaches to metaphor. Among the writers there discussed, in addition to Goodman, are Martin Foss, Monroe Beardsley, William P. Alston, I. A. Richards, Max Black, and Paul Henle.

74

In routine projection, habit applies a label to a case not already decided. Arbitrary application of a newly coined term is equally unobstructed by prior decision. But metaphorical application of a label to an object defies an explicit or tacit prior denial of that label to that object. Where there is metaphor, there is conflict: the picture is sad rather than gay even though it is insentient and hence neither sad nor gay. Application of a term is metaphorical only if to some extent contra-indicated.[2]

However, metaphorical truth, as distinct from simple falsehood, requires further that there be "attraction as well as resistance – indeed, an attraction that overcomes resistance."[3] To describe the picture as sad is to offer a true characterization capable of surviving conflict with the picture's insentience, which implies that it is not sad. "Nothing can be both sad and not sad unless 'sad' has two different ranges of application. If the picture is (literally) not sad and yet is (metaphorically) sad, 'sad' is used first as a label for certain sentient things or events, and then for certain insentient ones."[4] How is metaphor then distinguished from ambiguity, also characterized by different ranges of application for a given term?

Applying the term "cape" to a body of land on one occasion and to an article of clothing on another is using it with different and indeed mutually exclusive ranges but is not in either case metaphorical. How, then, do metaphor and ambiguity differ? Chiefly, I think, in that the several uses of a merely ambiguous term are coeval and independent; none either springs from or is guided by another. In metaphor, on the other hand, a term with

2 Goodman, *Languages of Art*, p. 69. As T. Cohen has pointed out, the formulation given here conflicts both with other passages in *Languages of Art* and with plausible examples. (See Cohen,"Notes on Metaphor," *Journal of Aesthetics and Art Criticsm*, 34 [1976], 258–9.) Goodman's main point is, however, not that the literal reading of a sentence is false if its metaphorical reading is true, but rather that the latter reading of a label involves an extensional shift. In other words, metaphorical application of a label to an object defies a prior denial of that label to some object satisfying the same application (or a prior denotation of some object denied the same application).
3 Goodman, *Languages of Art*, pp. 69–70.
4 Ibid., p. 70.

an extension established by habit is applied elsewhere under the influence of that habit; there is both departure from and deference to precedent. When one use of a term precedes and informs another, the second is the metaphorical one.[5]

The process by which one use of a term "guides" or "informs" another requires further interpretation. Goodman introduces the notions of "schema" and "realm," a schema consisting in a set of alternative labels, and a realm consisting of "the objects sorted by the schema – that is, of the objects denoted by at least one of the alternative labels." The underlying point is that

> a label functions not in isolation but as belonging to a family. We categorize by sets of alternatives. Even constancy of literal application is usually relative to a set of labels: what counts as red, for example, will vary somewhat depending upon whether objects are being classified as red or nonred, or as red or orange or yellow or green or blue or violet. What the admitted alternatives are is of course less often determined by declaration than by custom and context.[6]

Now in metaphor, says Goodman, we typically see a change in the realm of a label as well as a change in its range or extension. "A label along with others constituting a schema is in effect detached from the home realm of that schema and applied for the sorting and organizing of an alien realm. Partly by thus carrying with it a reorientation of a whole network of labels does a metaphor give clues for its own development and elaboration."[7]

The suggestion here is that the new application of a metaphorical label is guided, in part, by its place in the whole schema, which is itself transferred in a way that reflects its prior use: "A set of terms, of alternative labels, is transported; and the organization they effect in the alien realm is guided by their habitual use in the home realm."[8]

5 Ibid., pp. 70–1.
6 Ibid., 71–2.
7 Ibid., p. 72.
8 Ibid., p. 74.

As to how such guidance operates, Goodman offers no general account. He emphasizes the fact that the free transfer of a schema nevertheless yields determinate judgments:

> We may at will apply temperature-predicates to sounds or hues or personalities or to degrees of nearness to a correct answer; but *which* elements in the chosen realm are warm, or are warmer than others is then very largely determinate. Even where a schema is imposed upon a most unlikely and uncongenial realm, antecedent practice channels the application of the labels.[9]

This is, however, just to describe the main phenomenon that concerns us, that is, the success that may accompany metaphorical communication. Granted that freely transferred schemata yield determinate judgments, the problem is to explain how. It is Goodman's response to this problem that I interpret as suggesting a contextual approach. For he resolutely resists the provision of a general answer, offering instead illustrations of a variety of metaphoric processes.

Thus, he suggests that the guidance given by past uses may, in certain cases, derive not from the literal but from the metaphorical application of the term in question: "Perhaps, for instance, the way we apply 'high' to sounds was guided by the earlier metaphorical application to numbers (via number of vibrations per second) rather than directly by the literal application according to altitude."[10]

Further, he suggests that guidance may derive not only from the past applications of a label, whether literal or metaphorical, but also from its past exemplifications (literal or metaphorical). In this connection, he refers to E. H. Gombrich's game of "ping" and "pong." The object of the game is to apply these nonsense words to pairs of objects, and the result for many pairs is surprisingly determinate. Gombrich writes:

9 Ibid.
10 Ibid., pp. 74–5.

If these [words] were all we had and we had to name an elephant and a cat, which would be ping and which pong? I think
the answer is clear. Or hot soup and ice cream. To me, at least,
ice cream is ping and soup pong. Or Rembrandt and Watteau?
Surely in that case Rembrandt would be pong and Watteau
ping.[11]

The guidance underlying the determinate responses in these
examples cannot derive from the past denotation of the words in
question, since they have had no denotation at all. Goodman's
idea is that they have, however, exemplified certain properties or
predicates, and that they now take over the denotation of the
latter:

The application of these words looks back not to how they have
been used to classify anything but to how they have themselves
been classified – not to what they antecedently denote but to
what they antecedently exemplify. We apply "ping" to quick,
light, sharp things, and "pong" to slow, heavy, dull things because "ping" and "pong" exemplify these properties.[12]

Since "ping" and "pong" have had no prior denotation, there can,
of course, be no metaphor involved in their new applications in
the game. But guidance by past exemplification may also affect
the reassignment of a denoting label, and here the effect will be
metaphorical.

Still, the foregoing suggestions do not account for all cases or,
indeed, for all relevant aspects of metaphorical transfer. That
guidance derives from a prior metaphorical application may help
explain the present metaphor (as an elliptical instance of such
application), but hardly the earlier one. That exemplification may
play a role is illuminating, but in the case of "ping" and "pong" at
least, it is *metaphorical* exemplification that is presupposed: "Ping"
is not literally light and sharp, nor is "pong" literally heavy and
dull; such cases assume certain metaphors in explaining others.

11 E. H. Gombrich, *Art and Illusion* (New York, Pantheon 1960), p. 370.
12 Goodman, *Languages of Art*, p. 75.

Further, the primary case of guidance through past literal application is itself assumed but not explained.

Goodman himself, having given us his account of the directive effect of past exemplifications, continues as follows:

> The mechanism of transfer is often much less transparent. Why does "sad" apply to certain pictures and "gay" to others? What is meant by saying that a metaphorical application is "guided by" or "patterned after" the literal one? Sometimes we can contrive a plausible history: warm colors are those of fire, cold colors those of ice. In other cases we have only fanciful alternative legends. Did numbers come to be higher and lower because piles grow higher as more stones are put on (despite the fact that holes go lower as more shovelfuls are taken out)? Or were numerals inscribed on tree trunks from the ground upward? Whatever the answer, these are all isolated questions of etymology.[13]

Etymological or not, such occasionally "plausible histories" suitable to their respective contexts are all that Goodman offers to supplement the incomplete prior account of metaphoric processes. Can anything more be provided? "Presumably," he writes, "we are being asked, rather, for some general account of how metaphorical use of a label reflects its literal use." He admits that there has been "suggestive speculation" on this question, referring, for illustration, to the view that the literal use of many terms has been narrowed from an initially wider range, an apparently new metaphorical application being thus often merely a recovery of the earlier territory. Nevertheless, he concludes that such a view "obviously does not explain the metaphorical applications of all or even most terms. Only rarely can the adult adventures of a label be thus traced back to childhood deprivations."[14]

We have then an incomplete account of various processes operative in metaphoric transfer, and a suggestion of various plausible histories, together with the intimation that additional histories may be produced for individual contexts. Beyond that, Goodman

13 Ibid., p. 76.
14 Ibid., pp. 76–7.

maintains that no general theory of guidance can be offered. In particular, no general answer is to be sought in the notion of similarity:

> Is saying that a picture is sad saying elliptically that it is like a sad person? . . . But the simile cannot amount merely to saying that the picture is like the person in some respect or other; anything is like anything else to that extent. What the simile says in effect is that person and picture are alike in being sad, the one literally and the other metaphorically. Instead of metaphor reducing to simile, simile reduces to metaphor; or rather, the difference between simile and metaphor is negligible. Whether the locution be "is like" or "is," the figure *likens* picture to person by picking out a certain common feature: that the predicate "sad" applies to both, albeit to the person initially and to the picture derivatively.[15]

Is there, then, no general sort of similarity between the things a term applies to literally and the things it applies to metaphorically? Goodman suggests the same question might well be asked about the things a term applies to literally. In what way must all (literally) green things, for example, be similar?

> Having some property or other in common is not enough; they must have a *certain* property in common. But what property? Obviously the property named by the predicate in question; that is, the predicate must apply to all the things it must apply to. The question why predicates apply as they do metaphorically is much the same as the question why they apply as they do literally. And if we have no good answer in either case, perhaps that is because there is no real question.[16]

2 REMARKS ON CONTEXTUALISM

It is perhaps worth noting that Goodman's use of "metaphor" (like that of a good deal of the relevant literature) vacillates be-

15 Ibid., pp. 77–8.
16 Ibid., p. 78.

tween a very broad interpretation, in which it covers virtually all figures of speech, and a narrow interpretation, in which it represents a figure closely akin to simile. The general notion of schematic transfer covers a wide variety of figurative expressions, and Goodman indeed proposes an organization of this variety in a section of his discussion entitled "Modes of Metaphor."[17] On the other hand, in his criticism of the theory of metaphor as elliptical simile, he rejects the reduction of the former to the latter in favor of the view (quoted earlier) that "the difference between simile and metaphor is negligible." The ambiguity deserves attention but is perhaps theoretically harmless once remarked. Figurative expressions may well be profitably treated as a group under the heading of schematic transfer; those of the group with relatively clear bases of transfer having been segregated, the particularly difficult remainder associated with simile wants special attention and has, indeed, been the focus of most theoretical discussions.

A basic question about Goodman's treatment concerns the argument he offers against the reduction of metaphor to simile. Considering the idea that to say a picture is sad is to say elliptically that it is like a sad person, Goodman remarks that the simile cannot be taken merely to assert that the picture is like the person in some way or other. Indeed, he says:

> What the simile says in effect is that the person and picture are alike in being sad, the one literally and the other metaphorically. . . . Whether the locution be "is like" or "is", the figure *likens* picture to person by picking out a certain common feature: that the predicate "sad" applies to both, albeit to the person initially and to the picture derivatively.[18]

The problem with this argument, however, is that metaphor is a subcase of ambiguity: Thus, while "sad" may reasonably be described as a single *label,* it can hardly be described as a single *predicate,* for so to describe it would imply a single extension for

17 Ibid., p. 81 ff.
18 Ibid., pp. 77–8.

the label in question. Nor, a fortiori, can it be said that the likeness ascribed by the simile under consideration consists in the sharing of the common predicate "sad," since there is no such common predicate. It follows, finally, that the simile cannot be construed after all as saying (univocally) that person and picture are alike in being sad.

It might be suggested that the effect of this argument may be achieved without appeal to the single predicate "sad": The common feature in question may be just that the label "sad" (ambiguous though it may be) applies to both person and picture. This suggestion is itself difficult, however. For rather than merging simile with metaphor, as intended by the original argument, it would now rather merge simile with ambiguity in general. Similes would, in effect, be authorized to liken objects if only referred to by divergent replicas. The child camper would properly be said to be like an elephant, since each is correctly described by some replica of "has a trunk"; the garment would be considered like the stretch of coastline, each being rightly labeled "a cape." Similes would derive from etymological accidents generally rather than from the closer relations associated with metaphor, narrowly speaking. The line between simile, as envisaged in the original argument, and punning would become blurred (puns would generate similes).

Nor is it possible to reconnect simile with metaphor by requiring not just the applicability of a shared label, but the applicability of such a label now literally, now metaphorically. For such an explanation would assume the notion of metaphor to be accounted for. On the other hand, to require rather the applicability of a shared label now initially, now derivatively, would be independently inadequate. For accidentally ambiguous replicas are also applied at different times, and may also be related by strands of historical derivation. To separate out those strands peculiar to metaphor without circular reliance on the notion of metaphor would, I suggest, be practically impossible.

The notion that the predicate "sad," or even the mere label "sad," indicates a common feature underlying the simile or metaphor in question seems thus untenable. The proposal we have been considering was that both figures be understood as likening picture to person by picking out such a common feature. As to what similarity, further, underlay this feature itself, that is, what characterized the objects of the predicate "sad," Goodman replied, as we have seen, "There is no real question."[19] His strategy was thus twofold: (i) to interpret both the simile's explicit, and the metaphor's tacit, assertion of likeness as elliptical ("The simile cannot amount merely to saying that the picture is like the person in some respect or other; anything is like anything else to that extent"), acquiring determinacy through implicit reference to the ostensible sharing of the predicate "sad," and then (ii) to reject any further question as to a likeness presumed to form the basis for sharing this predicate. However, (i) must now be surrendered because of its vulnerable assumption of a common predicate "sad."

It is important, furthermore, to take note of a further difficulty with (i), relating to its assumption that the simile acquires determinacy through reference to one of its *contained* predicates. This idea is implausible independently of the difficulty just pointed out. For similes typically acquire determinacy through reference to predicates they do not themselves contain, even when contained ones are (unlike "sad") unambiguously applicable to the things said to be alike. To say, as educators have, that a child is like a young plant is to do much more than attribute youth to child as well as plant. It has been interpreted as conveying that there are further significant attributions to be made to both, for example, that child and plant are growing, that they require supervision, that they benefit from a controlled environment, that they pass through ordered developmental stages, and so on. The simile may indeed be made determinate or "filled in," but not in general through sole reference to contained predicates, even when unambiguously and appropriately applicable. Other predicates are brought in from without, in a manner that varies with context.

This point, interestingly enough, seems to be acknowledged in Goodman's own notion of "plausible histories" explanatory of

19 Ibid., p. 78.

certain metaphorical applications, for example, that "warm colors are those of fire, cold colors those of ice."[20] Here, despite (i), he does not say, with respect to warm colors and warm things, simply that they are alike in being warm, in the one case literally, in the other metaphorically. Rather, he imports the reference to an association with fire rather than ice as a further specification.

If (i) is to be dropped, is there an alternative strategy that will fulfill its basic motivation and preserve its contextualist features? It originated in the recognition that while metaphor may be taken as elliptical simile in that it omits the expression "like," simile itself is further elliptical in omitting determining specifications for this expression. Without further specification, the bare likeness affirmed by simile is trivial; (i) seemed to offer a general way of supplying such specification through appeal to a contained predicate. Without such appeal, is it possible to suggest another way in which the indeterminacy of both figures may be overcome?

The answer is yes. The simile does not say that one thing is like another merely in some respect, nor does it, as we have argued, uniformly say they are alike in respect of contained predicates. But these are not the only alternatives. The simile may say, rather, that things are alike in respects that are salient or important in the context in question. Such an interpretation rests heavily on contextual, sometimes controversial judgments of salience or importance; it is, at any rate, neither indeterminate nor trivial. Moreover, the process of specifying those respects thought to bear out the simile or metaphorical attribution is central to the practice of explication.

We have already illustrated, in the figure of the child and the plant, the manner in which predicates not contained in a given simile are imported so as to supply an interpretive basis for it. Clearly the same process holds for metaphor as well; whether we say the child is *like* a young plant or *is* a young plant makes no difference in this regard. Imported predicates are of course supplied in a way that depends upon an understanding of the context; there is no general (similarity, or other) formula for extract-

20 Ibid., p. 76.

ing them. Yet there may be limited principles helpful in the search for suitable predicates; acquired through experience or instruction, they may improve the interpretive abilities of readers.

A familiar formulaic approach to metaphor rests upon the principle of similarity supplemented by the proviso that the similarity be an important one. Such a principle escapes vacuity only through heavy dependence on context. This dependence is indeed a defect in a view that purports to offer a formula. It is, however, no defect in a view that rejects the very idea of a formula, insisting that metaphoric interpretation requires contextual judgment – not, indeed, of important similarities but of important predicates serving to define such similarities.

The version of contextualism here outlined yields, furthermore, an interpretation of the guidance afforded by literal applications to metaphoric ones. The earlier version, as we have seen, offered a view of metaphor resting on the notion of such guidance, but giving no explanation of it – indeed rejecting the question of why predicates apply as they do metaphorically. The present contextualism, resting on an understanding of the context for the suggestion of significant predicates, clearly requires also a grasp of the literal application of the term in question. For the metaphorical application is to be understood as attaching to things sharing satisfaction of contextually important predicates with those picked out by the literal application.[21] Knowledge of

---

21 Null terms (in literal application) require slightly different treatment, lacking things to satisfy them. The metaphorical application of "dragon" to persons can hardly be said literally to liken persons to dragons, there being no dragons. Goodman, in his *Ways of Worldmaking* (Indianapolis, Ind.: Hackett, 1978), p. 104, n. 10, points out that "since 'Don Quixote' and 'Don Juan' have the same (null) literal extension, their metaphorical sorting of people cannot reflect any literal sorting." He traces their metaphorical sorting to (literal) extensional divergence between parallel compounds of the terms, or differences in what these terms themselves satisfy and exemplify. "In sum, 'Don Quixote' and 'Don Juan' are denoted by different terms (e.g., 'Don-Quixote-term' and 'Don-Juan-term') that also denote other different terms (e.g., 'zany jouster' and 'inveterate seducer') that in turn denote different people."

Put in terms of mention-selection, the term with null literal extension

the context alone is not sufficient; literal application must also be taken into account. Such application does not determine metaphorical extension, but it contributes to this determination. In other words, it guides the interpretation of metaphor, when properly supplemented by contextual understanding.

3 METAPHOR AND EXPLORATION

In creating a metaphor one may surprise oneself. Much of the discussion of metaphor has been conducted with reference to contexts of communication, and a mistaken, though tacit, assumption has been prevalent; that is, that the producer of a metaphorical utterance has some special key to its comprehension that the hearer or reader can only struggle to find. In fact, the producer of any utterance, metaphorical or otherwise, may find it difficult or puzzling to interpret what has been said and be surprised by the result of reflection on the matter. The interpretive role with respect to any utterance is not incompatible with that of producer, even when the purpose of the utterance has been straightforward communication.

But a special word needs to be said about the uses of metaphor in primarily investigative or theoretical spirit. Here what is often involved is the exploratory or heuristic function of comparison. The theorist frequently does not know in advance the basis of the comparison he or she puts forth, but supposes, or guesses, that a certain general crossing of categories may turn out to be signifi-

mention-selects various descriptions of which some, important in context, may also characterize persons to whom reference is made. A person metaphorically described as Don Quixote is not literally likened to Don Quixote, nor does he share the satisfaction of important predicates with the literal Don Quixote; rather he satisfies certain important predicates constituting Don-Quixote-descriptions. Where a null term is rather the grammatical subject of a metaphorical attribution with a non-null predicate, for example, in "Don Quixote was a mule," "mule" is attributed metaphorically to those satisfying certain predicates mention-selected by "Don Quixote." And where, as in the metaphorical "Cinderella was an angel," both subject and predicate are (literally) null, some contextually relevant description mention-selected by "Cinderella" denotes persons satisfying certain metaphorical ascriptions mention-selected by "angel."

cant.[22] The metaphor embodying this guess does not signify a prior determination by the theorist of the predicates that are importable from the investigative context in substantiation of his utterance. On the contrary, the utterance itself serves as an *invitation*, to the theorist and others, to explore the context for significant shared predicates – new or old, simple or complex. The theorist offers not a declaration but a hypothesis: that there are important predicates in the relevant context for the "filling in" or specification of the metaphor – that there are, in other words, significant theoretical connections to be forged between the categories involved. The challenge is not to read a substantiated message, but to find or invent a significant description of nature.

The invitation presented by a metaphorical utterance may lead us to rethink old material in the light of new categorizations (the mind as an electronic computer) or to consider newly discovered phenomena in terms already available (black holes in space as vacuum cleaners). Whether the task be to incorporate the novel or to reorganize the familiar, metaphor often serves as a probe for connections that may improve understanding or spark theoretical advance.

The creative role of metaphorical utterance is again evident here. For it does not simply report isomorphisms, but calls them forth afresh to direct, and be tried by, further investigations. The happy outcome of such investigations is of course not assured beforehand. While certain connections flourish, others languish and die. An advance in comprehension is always an achievement, never a foregone conclusion.

It might thus perhaps be suggested that the theorist – or the producer of metaphor, more generally – does not know what he is saying ("the meaning" of what he is saying). For the metaphorical term used has an extension that the theorist typically cannot elucidate at the time of utterance, dependent as such elucidation may be upon contextually significant predicates determined as such

---

22 For a discussion of metaphorical "sort-crossing" in the context of theories of nature, see Colin Murray Turbayne, *The Myth of Metaphor*, rev. ed. (Columbia: University of South Carolina Press, 1970). See also the Appendix by Rolf Eberle, "Models, Metaphors, and Formal Interpretations," in ibid., pp. 219–33, esp. sec. 6, "Models as Tools of Discovery."

only in subsequent inquiry. The predicament is not, however, peculiar to metaphor, our literal attributions also gaining a theoretical refinement and determinacy through further investigations clearly not evident at the time of utterance. This situation is not likely to seem paradoxical unless we hold a firm division between meaning and fact. The process of finding out more about one's own meaning and finding out more about the world are, however, one and the same.

Chapter 7

Mainsprings of metaphor
(with Catherine Z. Elgin)

Josef Stern dismisses extensional theories of metaphor on the ground that substitution of coextensive terms does not always preserve metaphorical truth: "It may be a truism that the metaphorical depends on the literal, but this cannot mean that the extension of a term interpreted metaphorically simply depends on its extension interpreted literally."[1] True enough. But extant extensionalists are committed to no such thesis. To say that metaphor is determined extensionally is not to say that a term's metaphorical extension is determined solely or simply by *its* literal extension. Rather, the extensional references of associated literal and metaphorical expressions intertwine in fixing a term's metaphorical reference. Among the resources available to the extensionalist are the interpretations of related literal and metaphorical expressions,[2] secondary extensions,[3] mention-selection,[4]

"Mainsprings of Metaphor" appeared as Catherine Z. Elgin and Israel Scheffler, "Mainsprings of Metaphor," *Journal of Philosophy*, 84 (1987), 331–5.

Catherine Z. Elgin would like to thank the University of North Carolina Research Council for support of this project.

1 Josef Stern, "Metaphor as Demonstrative," *Journal of Philosophy*, 82, no. 12 (December 1985), 677–710, quoted at 683–4. Stern has replied to our arguments in the present chapter in his "Metaphor without Mainsprings," *Journal of Philosophy*, 85 (1988), 127–38.
2 Goodman, *Languages of Art* (Indianapolis, Ind.: Hackett, 1976), pp. 71–80.
3 Goodman, "On Likeness of Meaning," in *Problems and Projects* (Indianapolis, Ind.: Hackett, 1972), pp. 221–30; "On Some Differences about Meaning," ibid., pp. 231–8; *Languages of Art*, pp. 204–5.
4 Israel Scheffler, *Beyond the Letter* (London: Routledge, pp. 31–6, 142, n. 97; "Four Questions about Fiction," *Poetics*, 11 (1982), 279–84.

exemplification,[5] and complex reference.[6] There are no recipes for determining metaphorical meaning. But there are heuristics that guide our search, providing cues and clues about which aspects of the context and background might be relevant.

Stern notes that substitutivity of literally coextensive terms fails to preserve metaphorical truth. Although

> (a) Juliet is the sun

is true,

> (b) Juliet is the largest gaseous blob in the solar system

is false. Since the sun is the largest gaseous blob in the solar system, Stern concludes that extensionalism fails. He summarily dismisses secondary extensions, failing to appreciate the firepower they add to the extensionalist's arsenal.

A *secondary extension* of a term is the (primary) extension of a compound containing that term. The extension of "sun-description" is thus a secondary extension of "sun." But the extension of "sun-description" is not determined by that of "sun." Some sun-descriptions, such as those found in mythology, astrology, and ancient astronomy, are not true of the sun. Still, "sun-description" has a determinate extension – a particular class of words and phrases. And, although we have no rule for its instantiation, sun-descriptions are readily recognized. Indeed, this state of semantic affairs is common: We have no rule for the instantiation of "chair" either, but we recognize chairs without difficulty. To be sure, we probably cannot decide every case. We may be hard put to tell whether an odd linguistic construction is a sun-description and whether an odd material construction is a chair. But such difficulties do not impugn the determinacy of either extension.

5 Goodman, *Languages of Art*, pp. 50–8, 85–90.
6 Goodman, "Routes of Reference," in *Of Mind and Other Matters* (Cambridge, Mass.: Harvard University Press, 1984), p. 63ff.; see also, for further discussion of this and the previously mentioned devices, Catherine Elgin, *With Reference to Reference* (Indianapolis, Ind.: Hackett, 1983), pp. 146–54 and elsewhere.

Terms that agree in primary extension typically disagree in secondary extension. Although the primary extensions of "sun" and "largest gaseous blob in the solar system" are the same, their secondary extensions are not. "Apollo's flaming chariot," for example, belongs to the secondary extension of "sun," but not to that of "largest gaseous blob in the solar system." Literal meaning, Nelson Goodman suggests, is a matter of primary and secondary extension. So coextensive terms that differ in secondary extension differ in meaning.[7] It follows that, if metaphorical interpretation is a function of literal meaning, coextensive terms with different secondary extensions bear different metaphorical interpretations. Even if Romeo was an extensionalist, then, his assertion of (a) did not require him to accept (b). Extensionalists are committed to basing interpretation on nothing but extensions. But we are free to invoke any, and as many, extensions as we like.

A more perplexing problem is that the single term "sun" itself bears disparate metaphorical interpretations. Juliet is characterized as the sun because she inspires passionate love; Achilles, because he is prey to awful fury. Metaphorical meaning, it seems, attaches to tokens, not types.

But how do literally coextensive replicas – that is, tokens of a single type – differ semantically? Mention-selection provides the answer. In a mention-selective application, an expression refers, not to what it denotes, but to mentions thereof. "Unicorn" mention-selects unicorn-descriptions and unicorn-pictures; "sun" mention-selects sun-descriptions and sun-pictures. But not every sun-description need be mention-selected by a given inscription of "sun." Tokens occurring in a work of Ptolemaic astronomy, for example, mention-select "moving celestial body"; tokens in a work of Copernican astronomy mention-select "motionless celestial body." Literally coextensive replicas thus can, and often do, diverge in mention-selection. Still, mention-selection is extensional. There is a determinate class of expressions mention-selected by each token, and two tokens are co-

7 Goodman, "On Likeness of Meaning," p. 227.

mention-selective just in case they mention-select exactly the members of the same class.

Replicas that bear disparate metaphorical interpretations differ in mention-selection. Inscriptions of "sun" that apply meta-phorically to Juliet mention-select expressions such as "life-sustaining" and "beauteous"; those that apply to Achilles mention-select expressions such as "life-threatening" and "ter-rifying." The associations effected by the metaphorical applica-tion of an inscription are thus products of the literal mention-selective reference of that inscription. It is important to note that coextensive terms that differ in secondary extension also differ in mention-selection. Unlike "munchkin," "wizard" mention-selects "wise man." So "wizard" applies metaphorically to people to whom "munchkin" does not.

Metaphors achieve their effects through likening. This involves yet another mode of reference – exemplification. If a symbol both refers to and instantiates a label, it exemplifies that label. And, if two symbols refer to and instantiate exactly the same labels, they are coexemplificational. For example, a paint sample that both refers to and instantiates "vermilion" exemplifies "vermilion"; and separate paint samples that refer to and exemplify exactly the same labels – say, "vermilion," "flat," and "latex" – are coex-emplificational. Exemplification, like the other modes of reference we have considered, is thus extensional.

Things that do not ordinarily function as symbols come to do so by serving as samples of, and thereby exemplifying, labels they instantiate. This is the key to metaphorical likening. In calling Juliet the sun, Romeo highlights features she shares with the (lit-eral) sun. Through his characterization, he brings her to ex-emplify labels such as "glorious" or "peerless." So, in the simplest case, a chain of reference links the literal and metaphorical exten-sions of a term via their joint exemplification of a label. Thus, *Sol*, the literal referent of "sun," and Juliet, the metaphorical referent of "sun," are linked by their joint exemplification of the label "glorious." Longer and more complex chains may also connect literal and metaphorical subjects. Juliet might exemplify a label that exemplifies a label that . . . is exemplified by the sun. And the labels exemplified may be literal or metaphorical. Any number of chains can be operative at once. A rich metaphor is inexhaustible in that additional chains of reference between its subjects may yet be forged.

Context influences the interpretation of metaphors in several ways. Normally, a term is applied as part of a scheme of implicit alternatives. And a single expression might belong to a number of schemes. "Night," for example, can be opposed just to "day," or to "morning," "afternoon," and "evening." Moreover, the extension of a token of "night" varies slightly depending on which scheme is in play. Deep twilight belongs to the extension of "night" under the first scheme, to the extension of "evening" under the second. Settling the interpretation of a given token thus involves determining what kindred terms are, or might be, used in a given context. This is so whether the token functions literally or metaphorically. Rosalind is easily recognized as the referent of Romeo's "moon," for the way has been paved by his calling Juliet the sun.

Interpretation often depends on precisely what words are used and how they are described. This is largely a contextual matter. Romeo's previous Juliet-descriptions and Rosalind-descriptions, along with his conduct vis-à-vis the two women, reveal that his love for Juliet has totally eclipsed his affection for Rosalind. So his metaphorical comparisons of the two may reasonably be expected to favor Juliet. We do not need his explicit avowal of (a) to recognize Juliet as the proper referent of "sun," Rosalind as that of "moon."

Candidacy for exemplificational reference may also be circumscribed by contextual factors. The options for a correct interpretation of (a) are limited by the fact that it is uttered by a lovesick adolescent. We can expect the labels jointly exemplified by Juliet and the sun to be superlatives appropriate for describing objects of love and desire. They are unlikely to be predicates that belittle their referents. So, even though the sun is in fact a relatively insignificant star, contextual considerations exclude "insignificant" as a contender for joint exemplification. Whatever Romeo is getting at in calling Juliet the sun, he is not conceding that in the greater scheme of things, she is relatively unimportant. Such contextual considerations are plainly insufficient to determine exactly which labels are jointly exemplified. But, by restricting the candidate pool, they focus our search, directing our attention to a neighborhood in which a correct interpretation might be located.

Our primary objective in this chapter has been to defend extensionalism against Stern's dismissal. The account we sketch turns out to be stronger than the one Stern proposes. Unlike Stern, we invoke no intensional entities; so, our theoretical basis is more economical than his. And, if it accomplishes as much, the theory with the weaker basis is the more powerful. But, in fact, our theory explains more, and more that we particularly want to know, about metaphor. According to Stern, the most that semantics supplies for the interpretation of a metaphor is the advice: Look to context.[8] It does not explain how a metaphor likens the literal and metaphorical referents of a term. This, for students of metaphor, is a (perhaps *the*) crucial question. And it surely seems to be a question about how metaphors function linguistically.

By recognizing that exemplification is a mode of reference, that words and other symbols are among the referents of our terms, and that secondary extension and mention-selection depend on actual usage, not "lexical meaning," we can explain both metaphorical reference and metaphorical likening. Unlike Stern's theory, ours makes no use of a distinction between linguistic knowledge and collateral information. This strikes us as a good thing.

8 Stern, "Metaphor as Demonstrative," pp. 697–8.

Section IV

Symbol, play, and art

Chapter 8
Reference and play

I am concerned, in this chapter, with the phenomenon of play –
specifically that form of play in which a child seems to be engaged
in taking one thing for another, for example, apparently identifying a broomstick as a horse. In this situation, the child seems not
simply to be transferring the term "horse" to the broomstick –
providing a handy way of focusing attention on the stick by new
use of an old label. Nor does the child seem to be merely commit-
ting an error, taking the stick to be the sort of thing he has hitherto
called a "horse." The child seems to be doing something different
and more complex, attending to the stick via imaginative recourse
to horses or, perhaps, focusing on horses through special use of
the stick. In any case, the child's state of mind invites semantic
elucidation, that is, some account of how reference may be understood to function in such play.

Nor is the child's state of mind in play unrelated to other, and
perhaps weightier phenomena. Taking one thing for another is
what is seemingly involved in ordinary forms of reference to
works of art, in mimetic religious rites, in idolatry and word
magic, and in discussions of drama. We label a picture of a man
"man" rather than "picture of a man." In certain ancient mimetic
rites, ordinary mortals are apparently identified with the divine
beings addressed. In idolatry or, more generally, word magic, a

"Reference and Play" appeared in *Journal of Aesthetics and Art Criticism*, 50, no. 3
(Summer 1992), 212–16.

symbol is identified with a god or ascribed powers associated with the thing symbolized. In discussions of drama, actors are typically referred to by the names of the characters they portray. The common element in these various cases is the apparent taking of the symbol for the symbolized. For each such case, I have suggested a semantic interpretation based on mention-selection.[1] In this chapter, I apply this notion to the analysis of play.

1 GOMBRICH'S HOBBY HORSE

The topic of play identification has been intriguingly discussed by E. H. Gombrich in his essay, "Meditations on a Hobby Horse."[2] How shall we understand the child's apparent taking of the broomstick for a horse? Gombrich argues, first of all, that the child's attitude is not a feat of abstraction in which an equine form is first detached from its animal exemplars and then represented by the broomstick. "The very idea of abstraction as a complicated mental act lands us in curious absurdities. . . . Our mind," says Gombrich, "of course works by differentiation rather than by generalization, and the child will for long call all four-footers of a certain size 'gee-gee' before it learns to distinguish breeds and 'forms'."[3] This argument, one might protest, is not very convincing, since a broomstick, not being a four-footer, does not fall under the original general term "gee-gee" – eventually to be differentiated as one of its species. There is a jump from even the most generous "gee-gee" class to the broomstick, and it is this jump, beyond the reach of differentiation, that needs to be negotiated. How is it done?

Gombrich answers that the broomstick does not *represent* a horse; it itself *becomes* a horse. It is transformed from broomstick to horse when its "capacity to serve as a 'substitute'" is taken advantage of by the child.[4] The hobby horse does not

---

1 See Chapter 2, this volume.
2 E. H. Gombrich, "Meditations on a Hobby Horse," in *Meditations on a Hobby Horse* (London: Phaidon, 1963), pp. 1–11.
3 Ibid., p. 2
4 Ibid.

represent the most generalized idea of horseness. . . . If the child calls a stick a horse it obviously means nothing of the kind. The stick is neither a sign signifying the concept horse nor is it a portrait of an individual horse. By its capacity to serve as a "substitute" the stick becomes a horse in its own right, it belongs to the class of "gee-gees" and may even merit a proper name of its own.[5]

Indeed, the general assumption that an image "necessarily refers to something outside itself" has to be given up.

Nothing of the kind need be implied when we point to an image and say "this is a man." Strictly speaking that statement may be interpreted to mean that the image itself is a member of the class "man." Nor is that interpretation as far-fetched as it may sound. In fact our hobby horse would submit to no other interpretation.[6]

The child has, then, in fact created a horse. If this view seems extreme, it is nevertheless the main idea that Gombrich wants to press. "The idea that art is 'creation' rather than 'imitation' is," as he says, "sufficiently familiar," having been

proclaimed . . . from the time of Leonardo, who insisted that the painter is "Lord of all things," to that of Klee, who wanted to create as Nature does. But the more solemn overtones of metaphysical power disappear when we leave art for toys. The child "makes" a train either of a few blocks or with pencil on paper.[7]

Substitution, in Gombrich's view, is of course relative to function. The substitute, fulfilling some significant function of members of a class, joins that class.

The "first" hobby horse . . . was probably no image at all. Just a stick which qualified as a horse because one could ride on it.

5 Ibid.
6 Ibid.
7 Ibid., p. 3.

The *tertium comparationis*, the common factor, was function rather than form. Or, more precisely, that formal aspect which fulfilled the minimum requirement for the performance of the function – for any "ridable" object could serve as a horse.[8]

Similarly,

The clay horse or servant, buried in the tomb of the mighty, takes the place of the living. The idol takes the place of the god. . . . The idol serves as the substitute of the God in worship and ritual – it is a man-made god in precisely the sense that a hobby horse is a man-made horse; to question it further means to court deception.[9]

Creation may indeed precede communication, for Gombrich. The child inventor who made a horse

may not have wanted to show [it] to anyone. It just served as a focus for his fantasies as he galloped along – though more likely than not it fulfilled this same function for a tribe to which it represented some horse-demon of fertility and power. We may sum up the moral of this "Just So Story" by saying that substitution may precede portrayal, and creation communication.[10]

2 MEDITATIONS ON GOMBRICH

What does the child mean when he calls a stick a "horse"? Gombrich denies that the stick is "a sign signifying the concept horse" and proposes instead that in view of its ridability, the stick is capable of serving as a substitute and "becomes a horse in its own right." But how exactly is this proposal to be understood?

Does the child simply believe the stick to be ridable and, in that idiosyncratic sense alone, *therefore* a horse? There would then, contrary to Gombrich's suggestion, be nothing far-fetched about

8 Ibid., p. 4.
9 Ibid., p. 3.
10 Ibid., p. 5.

the child's belief taken thus; we adults can indeed agree that the stick is ridable, even if only in an extended sense. The child's creation of a horse would now amount to nothing more than his revision of the way "horse" ordinarily applies. Making a horse would amount merely to the child's changing the subject. Analogous remarks might be addressed to the idea that the child applies the term "horse" to the stick *metaphorically*, the metaphor resting only implicitly on the child's perception of the stick's ridability. For this metaphorical understanding of "horse" would be perfectly transparent even to adults; what Gombrich calls the child's creation of a horse would amount merely to his altering the reference of the word.

Moreover, the notion of the stick as substitute for a horse cannot be expressed, given only the revised understanding of the term. The stick is no substitute for a ridable object; it *is* a ridable object substituting for a horse, in the usual sense of the word. Nor does the stick substitute for a metaphorical horse; it *is* a metaphorical horse substituting for a horse, taking the word in its literal sense. The child must, in fact, appeal to the literal understanding of "horse" if he is to use the horse's ridability explicitly or tacitly as a function embracing the stick. The child must know what an ordinary train is to make one out of blocks. And if the stick is to "serve as a focus for his fantasies as he gallops along," these must be fantasies not just of *ridables* but of *horses;* the child fantasizes about horses, not sticks. Gombrich finally acknowledges the stick's capacity to *represent* for a tribe "some horse-demon of fertility and power"; thus does Gombrich, despite himself, invoke once again the notion of signification.

Suppose, then, that Gombrich is interpreting the child's belief otherwise. The child does not revise the usual understanding of the word "horse," nor apply it metaphorically to the broomstick. Rather, he believes of the stick that it has indeed literally become a horse, that "it belongs in the class of 'gee-gees'." From the child's point of view, though not from ours, he has indeed created a horse rather than just shifting the meaning of the word. Presumably, it is because the child's and the adult's beliefs are here in plain conflict that Gombrich puts quotation marks around the word "makes" when he writes, "The child 'makes' a train either of a few blocks or with pencil on paper." The child thinks he has made a train but we know better.

This way of taking Gombrich's proposal must reckon with the fact that he apparently does not limit it to young children alone; his extravagant belief-attributions apply also to adults, as his references to Leonardo and Klee suggest. Moreover, he says that "the idol . . . is a man-made god in precisely the sense that the hobby horse is a man-made horse," and he here does not put quotation marks around the word "man-made" to differentiate the adult idolaters' views from our own. Finally, he states, in a quite general way that ostensibly includes all of us, adults as well as children, "When we point to an image and say 'This is a man'," we are to interpret that statement to mean "that the image itself is a member of the class 'man'." This interpretation seems boldly to take the image of a man to be, literally, a man, and the creation of such an image to be an act of man-creation. And this consequence is evidently untenable.

The notion of substitution offered by Gombrich to explain the creation in question also harbors difficulties, to some of which we have already adverted. "Any 'ridable' object could serve as a horse," writes Gombrich, again putting quotation marks around the critical word. Is he thereby raising some doubt about the functional identity of horse riding and broom riding? He speaks of the "formal aspect [fulfilling] the minimum requirement for the performance of the function" but does not specify it. Is such function specifiable in advance or is it rather that in straddling the stick and galloping along, the child for the first time takes the stick as representing a horse and his own activity as representing the act of horse riding? Is the functional *"tertium comparationis"* any more than the formal one, initially there and available to be found, or is it rather imposed in the process of representation?

The notion of function, in any case, undergoes considerable attenuation as we move from broomstick riding to several of Gombrich's adult cases. "The idol serves as the substitute of the God in worship and ritual," says Gombrich, but is the ritual relation to an idol the same as the relation to a divine spirit? Is the ritual role of an idol, moved and handled by the priests or borne by the throng in procession, the same as that of the God?

Again, Gombrich states that a clay servant "takes the place of the living"; a man-image substitutes for a man. But what, in these cases, are the common functions on which the substitutions in question are presumed to be based? What minimal forms of behavior toward a living man do we transfer to a wallet snapshot of him?

Now, if on the basis of these and analogous considerations we reject Gombrich's view, we need to take seriously once again the idea of the broom as in fact a representation for the child. Of course, we can agree with Gombrich in giving up traditional views of such representation as based on imitation and formal identity – as well as ourselves raising doubts about his preferred notion of functional identity. The broomstick, we shall say, nevertheless stands for or refers to horses. But we need to face anew the question from which Gombrich's inquiry started. If the broomstick is not a horse, how is it that the child in play calls it a horse? How is it that, aware that the hobby horse is a mere stick, the child nevertheless refrains from referring to it as a stick representing a horse, but chooses instead to call it a horse? How shall we interpret the child's state of mind?

3 THE CHILD'S GROWING UNDERSTANDING

The broomstick, we have said, refers to horses. In galloping along on a broomstick, the child's fantasy is of riding a horse, not a stick, even though the child knows he is straddling a stick, not a horse. The child is merely using the stick to think of a genuine horse. The stick is a vehicle for the child's fantasy, not its target. What then does the child mean in calling the stick a "horse"?

We have already rejected the idea that he is simply applying the word "horse" metaphorically to the stick. For such application would amount simply to initiating a new denotation for an old word, thereby providing a novel way of referring to the stick. If it be objected that the literal sense of a metaphorical reference continues to be recalled, it must be insisted that such recall is short-lived. When a metaphor dies, such recall evaporates, leaving only a new literal reference. In the present instance, the reference would be to the stick alone; there would be no reference to horses as initially understood, no reflection of the fact that the child's focus is not on the stick but on horses, literally taken. Contrary to Gombrich, the child is not creating a horse literally, nor even metaphorically.

Can we combine the notion of metaphor with that of reference *by* the stick to horses? Here, Goodman's idea of metaphorical exemplification suggests itself. Exemplification is the relation of a sample to a label that applies to it and to which it refers – for example, the relation of a paint chip in a hardware store to the color label it satisfies. Exemplification is selective; the sample does not refer to every label that applies to it. The size or shape of the paint chip, for instance, is not referred to by the chip, though truly belonging to it. To exemplify a label, the sample must satisfy as well as refer to it.

Now, the term "horse," taken literally, does not apply to the broomstick. Thus, the stick cannot exemplify the label "horse," taken literally. However, "horse" can be deemed to apply to the stick metaphorically as we have already suggested, and further-more, the stick can be taken as exemplifying "horse" understood metaphorically. That is, the stick refers to the metaphorical "horse" label truly applying to it. Thus, we have interpreted the child's calling the stick a horse in such a way as to reflect the fact that the child's fantasy focuses on the horse, not the stick: The stick can be called a horse because it is indeed metaphorically a horse. But the stick does not simply *satisfy* the metaphorical "horse" label; it is itself also a symbol – referring back to the metaphorical "horse" label that denotes it. In employing this sym-bol, the child is thus led to think of its metaphorical "horse" referent.

There is, however, a flaw in this line of thought. We have re-marked that the child is using the stick to think of a genuine horse. But to refer to "horse" taken metaphorically is to refer to a label denoting not literal horses but rather sticks. The fact that a metaphorical "horse" label has non-coextensive literal replicas is no remedy for this situation. For if we were to allow the stick to refer to those replicas, we should need to allow samples to refer generally to non-coextensive replicas of the labels truly applying to these samples. A child's camp trunk would exemplify not only "trunk" labels as used in luggage stores, but also "trunk" labels as applied by zookeepers to elephants. Ambiguity would reign supreme. Thus, this proposal fails to bridge the gap between the stick and the literal horse, which is the focus of the child's thought. We have rather moved in a circle from the stick back to the stick.

Let us start afresh. Contrary to Gombrich, let us take it that the broomstick indeed signifies, stands for, or denotes horses. It is a horse-mention, along with pictures of horses, statues of horses, and descriptions of horses. Understanding the stick as a horse-mention enables us to use it as a device for focusing on horses. Now, adults can distinguish two ways of referring to mentions, one via denotation, the other via mention-selection. Each one of the preceding horse-mentions may thus be denoted by such compounds as "horse-representation," "picture of a horse," and the like. Alternatively, each may be captioned, that is, referred to mention-selectively as "horse."[11]

Were the child to call the stick "horse" mention-selectively, or to use the term as short for "horse-representation," the problem we are dealing with would be solved. We should understand why the child calls the stick a "horse" while at the same time explaining how the stick, functioning as denotative symbol, serves to focus the child's attention on horses rather than on itself. But, for the young child at least, these conceptions may seem to be too sophisticated. It is the objection against oversophisticated attributions to the child that, perhaps, motivates Gombrich's initial quest for a simpler account. If we share Gombrich's qualms on this score, can we then save the germ of the idea under consideration while simplifying our conception of the child's mental process?

We need to avoid supposing that the child already has the adult distinction between denotation and mention-selection or even that he is within short reach of it. Instead, let us suppose that the child does not at the outset recognize the distinction. He thus applies a term indifferently to its instances and, concurrently, to its companion signs. Thus, "horse," for the child, applies to horses

---

11 See Chapters 2 and 3, this volume.

but also, and equally, to pictures of horses and to "horse"s. The child does not, in short, acknowledge our distinction between the denotative and the mention-selective reference of symbols.

The child is not only willing to call a horse a "horse," but also to call a horse-representation, for example, a broomstick, a "horse." A horse-picture is thus for the child just another horse – indeed, a member of the class of things that may properly be called "horse." But this concession to Gombrich's insight must be qualified by recognizing that the class in question is considerably wider than that associated with the denotation of the term as used by adults. For it comprehends what *we* should call horses as well as what *we* should call horse-mentions. In making what the child calls a horse out of a broomstick, he need do no more than take it to be what *we* would describe as a horse-representation. From our point of view, some of the things he calls horses *represent* other of these things.

This phase of the child's understanding is, however, unstable. The child is under pressure to alter his understanding, since brooms are denied horsehood by the adults in his milieu. In the process of acquiring the conventional term "horse" and strengthening his grasp of it, the child is also continuing to learn the range of its complement term "nonhorse." Hence, the child is under pressure to agree with the adults in denying that the broom is a horse.

A first strategy the child may adopt to cope with such pressure is to divide the large group of things that he is willing to call "horse" into *real horses* and *pretend horses*. The child can then interpret the adults' denial that the broom is a horse as merely denying that it is a real horse, allowing that it is nevertheless a horse of the pretend variety. The child now takes pretend horses as *kinds* of horses. Of course, a pretend horse does not breathe or eat hay or gallop, but it is, in these respects, just different from other sorts of horses. After all, brown horses differ from black horses, Arabian horses from Elberfield horses, and so forth; broomsticks are just another kind.

This strategy defines my conjectured second phase of the child's understanding, and it may for awhile serve to resist the pressure of the adult denial, especially if the adult concedes that the broomstick is not a real, but only a pretend horse, and leaves it at that. But the pressure will resume once the adult has the occasion and the will to elaborate. For the adult will then insist that the pretend horse is no horse at all; it is no more a kind of horse than a decoy duck is a species of duck or a would-be doctor is a sort of medical specialist.

Succumbing to such pressure, the child finally separates horses from horse-representations, of which the broomstick is one. The stick is now conceded to be no horse at all, though acknowledged as representing a horse. The child has now, in effect, distinguished the denotative range of the conventional adult term "horse" from that of the conventional adult compound "horse-representation." In this phase, when he calls the broomstick a "horse," the force of the child's reference is quite different from that of his initial understanding. It is now mention-selective, in effect captioning the broomstick by use of a word for its putative represented object, much as we might caption a tree-picture "tree."

With the dawning of the fundamental distinction between denotation and mention-selection come various devices for fixing it in mind – including the use of explicit compounds of terms to *denote* members of their respective ranges of *mention-selection*. Such compounds are available when special care is to be taken, even though they may not be required in ordinary use.

Even after the basic distinction has become available, error is of course still possible. Special care may guard against it or eliminate it after the fact by recourse to the distinction, which is now part of the mental repertoire. But the blurring of the distinction remains a permanent hazard to which we all remain subject.

To return to my conjectural story, the child's broomstick continues to grow in fantasy: As Gombrich points out, the stick may acquire eyes, mane, ears, reins, and so on.[12] That is to say, "eyes," "mane," "ears," and "reins" may, in terms of our recent analysis, be supplied with suitable objects for mention-selection. A way of representing begins to take over and connect with other instances and applications. A clustering of mention-selections grows in which member captions interact creatively with one another to

12 Gombrich, *Meditations*, p. 5.

form families of representations, the stick and its addenda transformed into a rich symbolic display. The child at this stage, no matter what his or her actual age, has discovered the constructive possibilities of play.

4 FANTASY AND CREATIVITY

Gombrich speaks of the hobby horse as a focus for the child's fantasies as he gallops along. The child, as I earlier noted, fantasizes riding on a horse, not a stick, even though he knows that he is straddling a stick, not a horse.

The question that I now ask is, Why does the child need the stick as a focus at all? If his fantasy can overcome the patent fact that he is riding a mere stick rather than a horse, why cannot he simply fantasize that he galloping on a real horse, even without the stick as a focus? Certainly, in night dreams as well as daydreams we are caught up in fantasies without any physical activities to serve as their vehicles. The simple answer is that there is indeed no necessity for artifacts as vehicles for fantasy. But, where available, they serve additional functions in the service of imagination and creative thought.

For one thing, they provide stable sources for fantasy, which is otherwise fleeting, transient, and sporadic. The broomstick, as horse-representation, is an available and regular device for calling horses to mind, no less than is the case with a picture of a horse, or a description of a horse. Fantasy about horses need not be altogether internally generated and spontaneous, since it may be evoked by an independent physical representation.

Second, the character of such representation itself opens up possibilities for allied representations. As noted earlier, a new process of representation reverberates throughout our procedures of representation, affecting our view of other represented objects as well. To label a broomstick, via mention-selection, as *horse* is, as we have seen, to suggest ways of representing such equine addenda as eyes, mane, ears, reins, and so on. The initial mention-selection of the stick as *horse* is thus not inert and self-enclosed. It channels the creation of further representations as well, thus feeding the imagination in unforeseen ways.

Finally, to reassign the broomstick's function, even for limited intervals, from that of utilitarian instrument of housecleaning to that of horse-representation, is a significant act. It pries off the stereotypical characterization of the broomstick and stimulates a different perception of it, while at the same time encouraging us to view horses with new eyes. It thus helps to unstiffen our semantic rigidities and our perceptual pieties. To transform our view of objects, allowing us to see one thing as another, is a prime feature of creativity in play, and also in that sophisticated play which is art.

Chapter 9

Art, science, religion

Unlike science and art, science and religion have been at war. The very title of Andrew Dickson White's classic of 1910, *A History of the Warfare of Science with Theology in Christendom*,[1] epitomizes the dimensions of such conflict. In a lecture entitled "The Battlefields of Science," which preceded the publication of his book, White upheld the thesis that

> in all modern history, interference with science in the supposed interest of religion, no matter how conscientious such interference may have been, has resulted in the direst evils both to religion and to science, and invariably; and, on the other hand, all untrammeled scientific investigation, no matter how dangerous to religion some of its stages may have seemed for the time to be, has invariably resulted in the highest good both of religion and of science.[2]

1 CONFLICTS OF SCIENCE AND RELIGION

Nevertheless, as White's own massive two volumes testify, the conflicts between science and religion have been both continuous and intense, with science scoring a brilliant series of conquests.

"Art, Science, Religion," was first published in French as "Art, Science, et Religion," *Les Cahiers du Musée National d'Art Moderne*, 41 (Automne 1992), 45–53.
1 Andrew Dickson White, *A History of the Warfare of Science with Theology in Christendom*, 2 vols. (New York: D. Appleton, 1910).
2 Ibid., p. viii.

"In spite of ignorance, folly, and passion," wrote the historian of science William Dampier, "the scientific method has won field after field since the days of Galileo. From mechanics it passed to physics, from physics to biology, from biology to psychology, where it is slowly adapting itself to unfamiliar ground. There seems no limit to research," continued Dampier, "for, as has been well and truly said, the more the sphere of knowledge grows, the larger becomes the surface of contact with the unknown."[3]

Since the rise of modern science, a familiar scenario has repeated itself over and over. Religion has first seen itself threatened by some new scientific finding or theory and has forcibly opposed it. Thereafter it has sought to minimize the threat either by reinterpreting one or another of the elements in conflict or by retreating into a supposedly special province of thought immune to scientific criticism. Finally, having neutralized the initially offending doctrine, it has ended by accepting it or, indeed, proclaiming its truth. The names of Bruno, Copernicus, and Galileo spring to mind as the most celebrated examples, and Darwin, Lyell, and Freud follow soon after.

2 SCIENCE AND ART

No such warfare seems to characterize the historical relations of modern science and art, which seem, on the whole, to have been quite amicable. John Constable asserted that "painting is a science and should be pursued as an inquiry into the laws of nature. Why, then," he continued, "may not landscape painting be considered as a branch of natural philosophy, of which pictures are but the experiments?"[4] Commenting approvingly on these words of Constable, E. H. Gombrich declares that, "in the Western tradition, painting has indeed been pursued as a science. All the works of this tradition that we see displayed in our great collections apply discoveries that are the result of ceaseless experimenta-

---

3 Sir William Cecil Dampier, *A History of Science and Its Relations with Philosophy and Religion*, 4th ed. (Cambridge University Press, 1961), p. 500.
4 From Constable's fourth lecture at the Royal Institution in 1836. See C. R. Leslie, *Memoirs of the Life of John Constable*, ed. Jonathan Mayne (London: Phaidon, 1951), p. 323.

tion."[5] Art has, of course, also enjoyed the most intimate relations with religion. Yet in their different orientations to science, there is evidently a real difference between them: Religion and science have been at war while art and science dwell in peace. Why should this be so?

3 RELIGION COGNITIVE, ART AFFECTIVE?

One well-known traditional approach locates the answer within the semantic realm. It asserts that whereas religion is cognitive in its import, art is affective. Thus, religion purports to describe reality, as does science. Both are seekers after the truth, both cognitive in their aims and their doctrines. It is therefore understandable that emergent differences between them as to the truth concerning reality have engendered conflict. Art, on the other hand, and in contradistinction to the views of Constable and Gombrich, is not cognitive, but rather emotive in its import. Its function is to stimulate, express, or vent emotions rather than to describe reality. Its purpose is not theoretical but affective. It cannot, therefore, in the nature of the case, conflict with the descriptive assertions of science. Indeed, were art a cognitive enterprise, it would in fact be a mystery why it has *not* been at war with science, just as religion has been.

Two immediate problems confront this traditional view. First, if art is solely or primarily affective, how are we to explain the fact that artists have frequently thought of themselves in terms familiar to scientists? More generally, how are we to explain the significance of experimentation in art and the access of understanding that such experimentation affords? A second problem is this: How are we to explain the close affiliations of art with religion if, indeed, art is primarily affective whereas religion purports to describe reality? True, art as purely affective is compatible with religion as cognitive. It can no more challenge the dogmatic assertions of religion than it can threaten the theoretical propositions of science. But art is more than simply compatible in this way with religion; it enjoys an intimate association with religion that goes

5 E. H. Gombrich, *Art and Illusion* (New York: Pantheon Books, 1960), p. 34.

beyond its merely peaceable relations with science. How is this intimacy to be understood? The answers to both these problems require a couple of elaborations of the traditional view.

4 TWO ELABORATIONS OF THE TRADITIONAL VIEW

In the first place, both science and art are to be seen as, among other things, problem-solving enterprises, although their goals differ. In the course of developing true descriptions, science must invent and test hypotheses, make observations, and design experiments. In the course of creating objects that will appropriately stimulate, express, or vent emotions, art must also invent and try out various hypotheses, make observations, and engage in experiments. The problems in each case are different, but their respective problem-solving efforts are similar. It is therefore understandable that artists should view themselves as engaged in experimentation and seeking understanding even though their overriding purpose, to which experimentation and understanding are subsidiary, is to stimulate, express, or vent emotions. So runs one elaboration of the traditional view.

Second, while religion purports to describe reality, this is by no means the whole story. Religion also expresses and promotes a certain normative and emotional orientation to the reality it describes. It is, in this respect, no less affective than cognitive. Understandably, then, religion is thus not merely compatible with art, but intimately associated with it, using the affective power of art to reinforce its preferred emotive orientation and, conversely, lending itself to the expression of affective meanings independently conveyed by certain works of art. Thus runs the second elaboration.

When both elaborations of the traditional view are taken together, the bilateral relations of art with science and with religion are now accounted for. With the sciences, art shares its problem-solving ethos; with religion, it shares its capability for expressing and stimulating the emotive life. Thus elaborated, the traditional view needs again to be reckoned with. Despite art's problem-solving similarity to science, its overriding purpose is affective;

hence, it cannot come into conflict with the cognitive propositions of science. On the other hand, the major truth-seeking purpose of religion brings it into potential conflict with scientific views of the world – hence the warfare of science with religion.

This elaborated version of the traditional view is undoubtedly stronger than the original formulation. Nevertheless, it faces an insuperable obstacle – its characterization of art as affective in its primary purpose is untrue to the facts. The affective functions of art are not incompatible with its exercise of cognitive functions as well. Indeed, art typically functions affectively *through* its cognitive force, as well as cognitively *through* its affective force. The notion that the cognitive aspects of art are restricted to its problem-solving experiments in pursuit of primarily affective goals is simply incredible; it is an ad hoc device to save the emotive theory of art and has nothing else to recommend it.

Goodman has argued forcefully for a contrary interpretation of art, as driven by curiosity and aiming at enlightenment, employing the emotions themselves as instruments of cognition. "Representation or description," he writes,

> is apt, effective, illuminating, subtle, intriguing, to the extent that the artist or writer grasps fresh and significant relationships and devises means for making them manifest. . . . The marking off of new elements or classes, or of familiar ones by labels of new kinds or by new combinations of old labels, may provide new insight. . . . And if the point of the picture is not only successfully made but is also well-taken, if the realignments it directly and indirectly effects are interesting and important, the picture – like a crucial experiment – makes a genuine contribution to knowledge.[6]

Such discovery of new knowledge, as Goodman argues, is powered by the pursuit of understanding for its own sake. "The drive is curiosity," he writes,

> and the aim enlightenment. Use of symbols beyond immediate need is for the sake of understanding, not practice; what com-

---

6 Nelson Goodman, *Languages of Art* (Indianapolis, Ind.: Hackett, 1976), p. 33.

pels is the urge to know, what delights is discovery, and communication is secondary to the apprehension and formulation of what is to be communicated. The primary purpose is cognition in and of itself; the practicality, pleasure, compulsion, and communicative utility all depend upon this.[7]

The emotions themselves function cognitively in art. "The work of art," writes Goodman,

> is apprehended through the feelings as well as through the senses. Emotional numbness disables here as definitely if not as completely as blindness or deafness. Nor are the feelings used exclusively for exploring the emotional content of a work. To some extent, we may feel how a painting looks as we may see how it feels. The actor or dancer – or the spectator – sometimes notes and remembers the feeling of a movement rather than its pattern, insofar as the two can be distinguished at all. Emotion in aesthetic experience is a means of discerning what properties a work has and expresses.[8]

If the traditional view is thus finally defeated, and art reckoned as primarily cognitive, we confront once again, however, the problem with which we began. Why is it that religion alone conflicts with science, while art, as cognitive an enterprise as religion, does not?

5 DIFFERENT SYMBOLIC FUNCTIONS?

Perhaps, it may be suggested, the difference is to be sought in the particular symbolic functions involved in each case, rather than simply remarking that every one of our three enterprises is cognitive in character. In particular, let us recall that Goodman distinguishes denotation, exemplification, and expression as different modes of symbolic reference and that we may note a difference between science on the one hand and art on the other with respect to its dominant mode of reference. That is, denota-

7 Ibid., p. 258.
8 Ibid., p. 248.

tive import occupies a more central role in science than in art, while exemplification and expression are more salient in the arts than in the sciences. Assuming that religion is closer to science than to art in this regard, we may then be tempted to solve our initial problem as follows: Science and religion are at war since, for both, denotation is the primary vehicle of cognition, whereas art wars with neither since, while cognitive, it operates primarily through exemplification and expression.

But these contrasts are, first of all, matters of degree at best. Since, as Goodman remarks, "art and science are not altogether alien,"[9] it is no surprise to find that models in physics exemplify features critical to theory, that information in psychology and anthropology is often judged by its expressive features, and that a wide variety of works of art function regularly through denotation. While music and architecture, to be sure, do not typically function denotatively, the words employed in poetry and the novel do denote, and pictures frequently, if not always, represent in a manner characterizable as denotative. Second, it is not at all clear what the relevance of the supposed contrasts is thought to be. Even if, for example, denotation in art occupies a less dominant role relative to exemplification and expression than denotation in the sciences, there is still ample room for conflict between the two within the specific realm of denotation shared by both. Yet science wars with religion only and not also with art. But why?

6 CLAIMS TO TRUTH

Here, a new semantic idea suggests itself. That both science and art denote is not yet sufficient to show potential conflict between them. For conflict we also need claims to truth, embodied in contradictory statements. Denotation is, however, a function of general terms or predicates alone, and none of these either constitutes or implies a statement.

Now, science comprehends statements as well as predicates, and so does religion. They are therefore capable of asserting mu-

9 Ibid., p. 255.

tually contradictory statements, thus making conflicting claims to truth. But while pictures, which parallel the case of terms or predicates, may denote, they do not assert; there are, indeed, no pictorial parallels to statements, hence no pictorial claims to truth. Here, then, is a critical difference between pictorial art and religion, which explains their different orientations to science: Religion makes claims to truth, as does science, while pictorial art does not.

Is this matter so clear, however? Goodman has taken the view that "a picture makes no statement." "The picture of a huge yellow wrecked antique car, like the description 'the huge yellow wrecked antique car'," he writes, "does not commit itself to any of the following statements:

> The huge yellow wrecked car is antique
> The huge yellow antique car is wrecked
> The huge wrecked antique car is yellow
> The yellow wrecked antique car is huge,

or to any other. Although representations and descriptions differ in important ways, in neither case can correctness be a matter of truth."[10]

Now it is true that the definite description "the huge yellow wrecked antique car" is itself no statement, and therefore, does not logically imply any statement. Yet *any* atomic sentence formed by appending a predicate to this description implies an existence as well as a uniqueness claim, following Russell's theory of descriptions; that is, the claim that something is huge, yellow, wrecked, antique, and a car, and the claim that nothing else is huge, yellow, wrecked, antique, and a car. If either of these implied claims fails, we know, without any further information about the appended predicate, that the atomic sentence in question is false. The description, though it neither is nor implies any statement, is nevertheless peculiarly bound to certain statements in this way. True, if the description in question is supplemented not by a predicate but by the words "is not," the conjoined exis-

10 Nelson Goodman, *Ways of Worldmaking* (Indianapolis, Ind.: Hackett, 1978), p. 131.

tence and uniqueness claims are denied. But to add these words is tantamount not to predication but to quantification; it is to say in effect that there is no such thing as the huge yellow wrecked antique car. However, every case of supplementation by a genuine predicate to produce an atomic statement puts these claims into effect.

We have so far been discussing the singular description "the huge yellow wrecked antique car" and arguing its peculiar connection to certain statements. When, however, we turn from the *description* to a *picture* of a huge yellow wrecked antique car, it becomes impossible to apply the same argument, since there is no pictorial analogue of the singular description operator "the." Nevertheless, we might, in particular contexts, judge that a picture purports to denote a unique object and indeed succeeds in doing so. In such cases, we might suppose the picture to be peculiarly related to relevant existence and uniqueness claims, as in the case of descriptions. But would this be all and would it be enough? In the case of the description, the existence and uniqueness claims are implied by the full atomic statement whose content we understand. What is the parallel in the case of the picture? What does the picture, after all, say as a whole about the unique object it denotes? What statement is it presumed to be making?

Richard Rudner has, indeed, proposed the novel theory that "each symbol . . . in effect says that it refers to what it does in fact refer to." A picture of the Black Forest says (in Goodman's version of Rudner), "I depict the Black Forest." But if this is all the picture says, argues Goodman,

> what could constitute a false or wrong picture of the Black Forest? Under this criterion, whatever depicts the Black Forest counts as a true or right picture of it; for all the picture claims is that it does depict the Black Forest. A picture that does not depict the Black Forest does not claim to do so, and thus cannot be counted as a false or wrong picture of the Black Forest. To allow for wrong pictures, we would have to interpret a picture of the Black Forest as saying something more than that it depicts the Black Forest. But then we must ask "What more?";

we no longer have a clear general principle for unique correlation of a statement with a picture.[11]

A different idea suggests itself in connection with the referential notion of "representation as," which Goodman discusses in *Languages of Art.* "In general," he writes, "an object *k* is represented as a soandso by a picture *p* if and only if *p* is or contains a picture that as a whole both represents *k* and is a so-and-so picture."[12] That Winston Churchill is represented as a cigar smoker by a given picture is tantamount, according to this view, to the picture's being or containing a cigar-smoker-picture representing Churchill. Alternatively, that Churchill is represented as an infant by a certain picture is tantamount to that picture's being or containing an infant-picture representing Churchill.

Now in the first of these cases, the picture, though it is itself no statement nor literally implies any statement, may be taken as bound to the statement "Churchill is a cigar smoker" in a way perhaps analogous to what was said earlier about descriptions. That is to say, were this statement to be judged false while judging the picture to represent Churchill as a cigar smoker, the picture would be deemed to offer a nonfactual depiction of its subject. In the second case, the picture can be taken, in parallel fashion, as bound to the statement "Churchill is an infant," although, of course, the latter statement makes a claim to metaphorical rather than literal truth.

Here, we apparently have an answer to the question "What more?" earlier directed to Rudner's theory. For each of our Churchill-pictures is bound to more than just the claim that it depicts Churchill. It is further bound to the claim that Churchill is what he is depicted as being, which may or may not in fact be correct. The important point, however, is not correctness but the claim to correctness. That the claim is in the one case to a literal, in the other to a metaphorical, truth should not obscure the basic

---

11 Nelson Goodman, *Of Mind and Other Matters* (Cambridge, Mass.: Harvard University Press, 1984), pp. 97–8. See Richard Rudner, "Show or Tell: Incoherence Among Symbol Systems," *Erkenntnis,* 12 (1978), 129–151, 176–9.
12 Goodman, *Languages of Art,* pp. 28–9.

point that a statement is here, in effect, tied to a picture. To the extent that this point can be generalized, we are brought back once again to our original problem: If pictorial art is interpretable as bound to certain truth claims, as are science and religion, why does science war with religion but not with art?

The problem is of course heightened when we consider not only pictorial art but also verbal or literary varieties. For these varieties clearly make statements, both literal and metaphorical; moreover, even where the literal purport of such statements is false, the metaphorical purport may make claims to truth. This fact again brings art into potential conflict with science, yet no war ensues as it does when science confronts religion.

7 A RECONSIDERATION

These results suggest that we had better reconsider our starting points. For whether we take art to be noncognitive, as the traditional view claims, or cognitive, as we have recently urged, no answer to our original problem is forthcoming. We need to ask if our original problem is not, after all, misconceived.

Is it in fact true that art has enjoyed amiable relations both with science and with religion? Romantic nineteenth- and twentieth-century writers have assailed science as destroying the life of art and culture, while proponents of science have attacked effete aestheticism and decadence. Religious puritans of one or another stripe have, now and again, attacked the theater, dance, music, and graven images, while avant-garde artists have mocked the rigidities of religious piety. The divisions between art and science, on the one hand, and art and religion, on the other, have indeed run so deep as to have inspired a variety of social theorists with the goal of overcoming such cultural rifts in the name of social sanity.

It is true that both science and religion are not wholly confined to the verbal realm, that both require overt expression in tangible objects of the physical world – the one in experiment, the other in the sacra of religious symbolism – and that this brings them into collaborative contact with artist and artisan. But such contact does not wholly preclude conflict, even war. Following this line of thought, we seem driven to conlude that science is after all at war not only with religion but also with art, and religion is at war not only with science but with art as well. We need to give up our initial assumption that there is a conflict between science and religion alone. In fact, it seems, we have to contend not with a single conflict but with a war of all against all.

Nor does it mitigate this conclusion to point out that these latter conflicts are sporadic rather than continuous, that religion often dwells peaceably with art, and art peaceably with science. For the same holds of science and religion, which, despite the eruption of states of war on various occasions, also experience intermittent periods of irenic bliss. Is there, then, no difference to be noted? Is the question we have been pursuing based on mere illusion? Why is it the warfare of science and religion, in particular, that is so often salient in discussions of culture?

We have seen that the answer to this question does not, in any event, lie in semantic capabilities, that is, in supposed differences between art, science, and religion as regards their cognitive or symbolic powers. If religion makes statements, so in its own way does art. Both are ipso facto able to offer statements in conflict with science.

8 THE RELEVANCE OF AUTHORITY

It is perhaps, however, in the pragmatic rather than in the semantic dimension that an answer to our question may lie. That is, the social context of statement making in art differs from that of science and of religion. The mode in both science and religion, in a word, involves authority; the mode in art does not. The doctrines upheld by religion in a given community at a given time are those sanctioned by the relevant religious authority at that time. Analogously, the doctrines forming the corpus of science in a community at a given time are those upheld by the authority of expert scientific opinion at that time. It does not matter that religious authority is often more centralized within a religious community than that of science, that scientific authority is more diffuse. Nor does it matter that religious authority itself has variant embodiments in different religious communities. The principal point is that there is typically such a thing as authoritative religious doctrine in any such historical community and such a thing as expert scientific opinion within any discipline at a given juncture.

We are perhaps more accustomed to thinking of religion in connection with authority and perhaps uncomfortable with the notion of authority in the realm of science, where the free judgment of the individual scientist is supposed to reign supreme. No one has written more tellingly about the nature of authority in science than Michael Polanyi, who has emphasized not only the consensus of scientific opinion, but the fact that such consensus emerges out of individual judgment. "The consensus prevailing in modern science," he writes,

is certainly remarkable. Consider the fact that each scientist follows his own personal judgment for believing any particular claim of science and each is responsible for finding a problem and pursuing it in his own way; and that each again verifies and propounds his own results according to his personal judgment. Consider moreover that discovery is constantly at work, profoundly remoulding science in each generation. And yet in spite of such extreme individualism acting in so many widely disparate branches, and in spite of the general flux in which they are all involved, we see scientists continuing to agree on most points of science. . . . The harmony between the views independently held by individual scientists shows itself also in the way they conduct the affairs of science. . . . There is no central authority exercising power over scientific life. It is all done at a multitude of dispersed points at the recommendation of a few scientists who happen either to be officially involved or drawn in as referees for the occasion. And yet in general such decisions do not clash but on the contrary, can rely on wide approval. If scientists could not trust one another as informed by the same tradition, the processes of publication, of compiling text-books, of teaching juniors, of making appointments, and establishing new scientific institutions, would henceforth depend on the mere chance of who happened to make the decision. It would then become impossible to recognize any statement as a scientific proposition or to describe anyone as a scientist. Science would become practically extinct.[13]

Polanyi describes the common tradition of science as resting on chains of what we may think of as internal authority. Such internal authority is necessitated by the fact that

> nobody knows more than a tiny fragment of science well enough to judge its validity and value at first hand. For the rest he has to rely on views accepted at second hand on the authority of a community of people accredited as scientists. . . . What happens is that each recognizes as scientists a number of others by whom he is recognized as such in return, and these relations form chains which transmit these mutual recognitions at second hand through the whole community. The system extends into the past. Its members recognize the same set of persons as their masters and derive from this allegiance a common tradition, of which each carries on a particular strand.

The consensus of scientific opinion at any time is supported by the network of accredited associations forming the scientific community. "Anyone who speaks of science in the current sense and with the usual approval, accepts this organized consensus as determining what is 'scientific' and what 'unscientific'. When I speak of science, I acknowledge both its tradition and its organized authority, and," says Polanyi, "I deny that anyone who wholly rejects these can be said to be a scientist, or have any proper understanding and appreciation of science."[14]

Despite its individualism, then, science is embodied in institutions serving as arbiters of authoritative scientific opinion. This fact is indeed of crucial consequence for our problem. For it makes it possible to speak not just of this or that scientist as disagreeing with this or that churchman. It is the corporate conflict of science with religion that takes place when authoritative religious doctrine clashes with competent scientific opinion. Even

13 Michael Polanyi, *Science, Faith, and Society* (Chicago: University of Chicago Press, 1996), pp. 50–3.
14 Michael Polanyi, *Personal Knowledge* (New York: Harper, 1958, 1962), pp. 163–4.

where it is a single scientist who bears the brunt of the conflict, he or she represents the authoritative community of scientific investigators and experimenters.

Individual members of the religious community may have their private opinions, but they are aware of the demands of official doctrine and they recognize the authorities who make institutional decisions for the community. Nor do contemporaneous scientists vary, by and large, on matters of expert scientific consensus, even if such consensus changes, slowly or rapidly, over time and even if, as Polanyi argues, "every thoughtful submission to authority is qualified by some, however slight, opposition to it."[15]

When we turn to art, we find a striking contrast to both religion and science as just described. Art has no experts or doctrinal authorities to lay down corporate items of belief or make decisions for the community. The community of artists is in fact not a community of belief. Art has styles, to be sure, but these styles do not bind. They form the background for the training and discipline of budding artists, but those budding artists are not meant to confirm a consensus of artistic doctrine or to uphold the authority of expert artistic opinion. Their individualism means that they do not speak with one voice but with many. Thus, while there certainly *can* be a conflict between a given artist, or school of artists, with religion at a given time and place, there can be *no* conflict of art as a corporate structure, with religion, even if all extant artists then and there express religious heresies. For such a communal heresy would be distributive, not collective, de facto but not de jure. Similarly, this or that individual artist or group of artists may dissent from the expert scientific consensus of the day, but there can be no rift between art as such and science as currently embodied in authoritative scientific opinion, even if every artist were systematically to flout such opinion.

There is, to be sure, a sense of "authority" that is personal rather than institutional, the sense, noted by R. S. Peters, in which being *an authority* is to be contrasted with being *in authority*. Such personal authority "depends entirely," as Polanyi has said, "on

15 Ibid., p. 164.

the respect in which [persons may be] held by their admirers and followers, as is the case with poets or painters."[16] But the contrast between art and science is nevertheless firm. "The arts, like the sciences," writes Polanyi,

> are most alive in the process of renewing themselves; fame is earned in the arts, as in science, by creativity. But artistic originality involves as a rule more comprehensive changes of outlook than does originality in science, and tends to produce therefore more pronounced divisions of opinion between the innovator seeking to establish his authority, and the leaders of previously established art. . . . And of course . . . the arts are not, and never can become, systematically coherent after the fashion of sciences. There can, therefore, exist no . . . such firm consensus of opinion among them, as we have within the community of scientific specialists.[17]

It is a corollary of these points of contrast that science may be cumulative even if in fact it is subject to revolution and does not always accumulate, and that religious belief may similarly accumulate, even if in fact it is subject to schism and heresy. There is, in these respects, a quasi-linear ordering of states of corporate belief, by inclusion, in both science and religion. But not so with art. For corporate artistic belief does not exist, even though predominant stylistic features may be abstracted in given periods of artistic development. Such features do not, moreover, grow by accumulation. Artistic development indeed occurs, but its principle is not one of relative inclusion.

The individualism of modern art means that it does not engage in corporate war with science or with religion. But this is not enough to imply perfect peace. That there is no conflict of authoritative structures of consensus on both sides does not mean that there can be no wholesale attacks on artistic freedoms from the side of religion, or threats to the artistic imagination from a narrow construction of scientific truth or method. It does not

16 Ibid., p. 220, and R. S. Peters, *Ethics and Education* (London: Allen & Unwin, 1966, 1970), chap. 9, p. 239.
17 Polanyi, *Personal Knowledge*, p. 220.

mean that artists cannot promote pseudoscientific cults and spread superstition. Nor, as the case of Salman Rushdie indicates, does it mean that particular artistic works cannot be perceived as threatening religious beliefs. If the genuine warfare of science and religion stands out, it is because structures of authority on both sides are indeed at stake no matter what the particular causa belli. However, there are, alas, many other ways to disturb the peace. In place of corporate war, we often have a scatter of skirmishes, a rat-a-tat of raids and counterraids, intermittent invasions and guerrilla strikes. Not quite a war of all against all, but neither total harmony nor even truce.

Section V
Symbol and ritual

Chapter 10
Aspects of ritual

The treatment of ritual proposed here outlines multiple symbolic functions of ritual, which together serve to mark out a structure of historical time, space, and community. Patterns of ritual repetition, furthermore, bring performers' minds into regular contact with symbolized properties, thus influencing their concepts and sensibilities.

The focus on symbolic aspects is an act of abstraction. It must not be taken as denying the importance of the social functions of ritual, nor of the belief system that, in every case, provides its context and motivation. On the other hand, to abstract from such features in order to concentrate on the symbolism of rites draws special attention to their cognitive roles, that is, their roles in conceptualization and reference and, consequently, in shaping the mental sensibilities and habits of their participants.

1 THE DEVALUING OF RITUAL

The mere assignment of cognitive roles to rituals conflicts with its prevalent devaluation as a hindrance to spontaneous religious

"Aspects of Ritual" is drawn from "Ritual, Myth, and Feeling: Cassirer and Langer," Part I, Section 6 of my *Inquiries* (Indianapolis, Ind.: Hackett, 1986), pp. 41–51; and my "Ritual and Reference," *Synthese*, 46 (March 1981), 421–37. Portions of this chapter were also presented at the Peirce International Congress at Harvard University in 1989 and appeared in my *In Praise of the Cognitive Emotions* (New York: Routledge, 1991), pp. 62–8.

feeling. Thus, William James's *Varieties of Religious Experience* begins by dividing the religious domain into the institutional and the personal, proceeding thereafter "to ignore the institutional branch entirely." The sort of religion in which James is himself interested gives rise, as he says, to "personal not ritual acts, the individual transacts the business by himself alone, and the ecclesiastical organization, with its priests and sacraments and other go-betweens, sinks to an altogether secondary place. The relation goes direct from heart to heart, from soul to soul, between man and his maker."[1] Assimilated by James to institutional machinery that slows or obstructs the free flow of religious sentiment, ritual is here mentioned only to be dismissed.

It is true that where it has not been thus dismissed, ritual has been assigned not to feeling but to the contrasting realm of cognition – but with equally devaluing effects. For it has here been associated with myth – itself viewed as defective cognition, bad science, pathological belief. Whether a hindrance to religious emotion or an objectification of falsehood or illusion, ritual has not often been considered as serving properly cognitive functions.

2 CASSIRER AND LANGER ON RITUAL

Two recent thinkers may be considered pioneers of the symbolic treatment I offer: Ernst Cassirer and Susanne Langer. Cassirer proposes to redress the devaluative attitudes just described, interpreting mythical thought, always associated with ritual, as a positive stage in the development of science. Resting on a unity of feeling that views nature as "one great society, the *society of life*," myth perceives *physiognomic* rather than objective features – structuring a "dramatic world – a world of actions, of forces, of conflicting powers. . . . Mythical perception is always impregnated with these emotional qualities." This world is the first stage in the development of human thought, in turn overcome by the

---

1 William James, *The Varieties of Religious Experience* (New York: Random House, 1902, 1929), p. 30.

"world of our sense perceptions" which is, in its turn, succeeded by the generalizing concepts peculiar to the scientific understanding of the physical world. None of Cassirer's three stages is "a mere illusion," science does "not extirpate [its predecessors] root and branch," though it must abstract from them in order to attain the objectivity required for its own function.[2]

Though Cassirer does indeed deny that myth constitutes "a mere mass of unorganized and confused ideas" and affirms its role in structuring a world from which "empirical thought" has grown,[3] he sees its virtue to lie not in its own cognitive deliverances but in its giving way developmentally to an eventually maturing science. His defense of myth and ritual is limited by its underlying contrast of emotion and science, strengthening the dubious view that cognition is scientific or nothing and the equally dubious idea that scientific cognition is devoid of emotion.

Langer, unlike Cassirer, separates ritual from myth, associating myth with fantasy and dream, but relating ritual to religious feeling "bound . . . to set occasions, when the god-symbol is brought forth and officially contemplated." At first "an unconscious issue of feelings into shouting and prancing," the agitation evolves into "a habitual reaction . . . used to *demonstrate*, rather than to relieve, the feelings of individuals." The overt act has in this phase become a gesture – no longer a symptom of feeling but a symbol of it – denoting it and thus bringing it to mind. As an articulation of feelings, ritual produces "not a simple emotion but a complex permanent *attitude* . . . an emotional pattern, which governs all individual lives. . . . A rite regularly performed is the constant reiteration of sentiments toward 'first and last things'; it is not a free expression of emotions, but a disciplined rehearsal of right attitudes."[4]

---

2 Ernst Cassirer, *An Essay on Man* (New Haven, Conn.: Yale University Press, 1944), pp. 76–83.
3 Ibid., p. 76.
4 Susanne K. Langer, *Philosophy in a New Key* (New York: Penguin Books, 1942, 1948), pp. 122–24.

Langer, more clearly than Cassirer, separates the display of feelings from their articulation. As gestures, rituals are for her primarily symbolic or referential, denoting rather than evincing feeling. The feelings they denote record "man's response [to] the basic facts of human existence" as expressed by the sacred life symbols arising in myth. But, regularly repeated, the ritual reference to such responses in itself shapes attitudes and forms habitual dispositions.

Langer is certainly right, I believe, in emphasizing the formalization of ritual and its gestural, that is, its symbolic character. But her interpretation is too restricted both in its conception of the symbolic process itself and in its designation of the objects symbolized in ritual. For she thinks of the process as *denotation* strictly, and she conceives the objects to be, uniformly, *feelings*. Rituals may, however, symbolize anything, not just feelings; as Cassirer put it, "a dramatic world – a world of actions, of forces, of conflicting powers." And the process of symbolization need not be restricted to denotation but may encompass other forms of reference as well. Indeed, ritual is typically symbolic in several modes simultaneously, and gathers strength thereby. The oft-noted capacity of ritual to survive changes in doctrinal interpretation may stem just from being linked by diverse bonds of reference to objects. When one or more are cut, the others meanwhile hold fast. When one requires relocation under a new interpretive idea, the untying and retying process does not destroy the whole linkage. Thus it is that rituals change more slowly than creeds, often surviving even drastic alterations of doctrine and entering into new interpretive contexts without serious loss of vigor.

I now consider five modes of ritual symbolization or reference, beginning with three varieties proposed by Goodman in and for his study of the arts,[5] namely *denotation, exemplification,* and *expression,* and supplementing these with two further modes, that is, *mention-selection* and *reenactment,* which I suggest are peculiarly relevant to the interpretation of ritual. I shall, in general, make comparisons between ritual and the arts in an effort to bring out what is distinctive in ritual reference.

5 Nelson Goodman, *Languages of Art* (Indianapolis, Ind.: Hackett, 1968, 1976).

3 DENOTATION AND EXEMPLIFICATION

Ritual gestures may denote or represent historical occurrences or occurrences thought to be historical, they may portray expected occurrences or hoped-for contingencies, they may denote or purport to denote persons, gods, or things. They may perform this role through bodily movement, after the manner of mime, but not necessarily thus. They may also employ the voice in song or speech. Indeed, the range of ritual gestures includes that of verbal gestures – the recitation of formulas, blessings, prayers, incantations, and the like. Thus, any denotative role capable of being fulfilled by verbal means is to be counted as also within the repertoire of ritual reference. Objects employed in ritual may also function symbolically and, in particular, may stand for or denote in a wide variety of ways.

Not every ritual gesture denotes, but normally every such gesture has firm specifications or prescriptions that it must satisfy. These may be set out verbally and written down, or transmitted orally, or they may be understood in context – but that there is a right and a wrong way of execution is normally evident. Now, every successful performance is an example of the rite in question, that is, it literally exemplifies it. To say this is to say not only that it satisfies the relevant specifications for the rite in question, but that it constitutes a *sample* of it, thus referring to it. In this way, it lends itself to auxiliary use as a demonstration in the process of teaching the rite to learners.

4 RITUAL AND NOTATION

Are the specifications for rites fully notational, in Goodman's sense of the term? I cannot here discuss his technical requirements for notationality.[6] However, the main point for present purposes will be grasped by attending to the case of musical scoring as a notational system and noting Goodman's idea of the basic function of a score as "the authoritative identification of a work from performance to performance."[7] As he explains, "Not

6 Ibid., Chap. 4.
7 Ibid., p. 128.

only must a score uniquely determine the class of performances belonging to the work, but the score . . . must be uniquely determined, given a performance and the notational system."[8] The question is, then, whether rites are, or can be, scored.

Now, in a trivial sense, anything can be scored. Even painting, an art that is, in Goodman's terminology, *autographic* (i.e., vulnerable to forgery), can be supplied, as he points out, with a scoring system "assigning a numeral to each painting according to time and place of production."[9] The purpose of having a score is, however, to emancipate identification of works from reference to the history of production. This, the scoring system just mentioned fails to do. On the other hand, a different system that did in fact accomplish such emancipation for the case of paintings would violate the antecedent practice of identifying a work with the individual picture alone. For this reason, Goodman concludes that, for painting, a notational system cannot be devised that will be nontrivial, that is, will both accord with prior practice and be independent of the history of production.[10]

The case of rituals seems, however, quite different; antecedent practice does not identify a rite with an individual performance alone, but rather with an appropriate group of performances. To devise a scoring system that is not trivial, that is, that will not depend upon history of production and will yet mirror antecedent classification, seems thus theoretically possible, although certainly not a routine task. Indeed, the motivation for notationality in the case of ritual appears similar to that suggested by Goodman for certain of the arts:

> Where the works are transitory, as in singing or reciting, or require many persons for their production, as in architecture and symphonic music, a notation may be devised in order to transcend the limitations of time and the individual. . . . The dance, like the drama and symphonic and choral music, qualifies on both scores while painting qualifies on neither.[11]

8 Ibid., pp. 129–30.
9 Ibid., p. 194.
10 Ibid., p. 198.
11 Ibid., pp. 121–2.

Ritual, it would seem, qualifies on at least one, frequently on both, scores as well.

Let us remind ourselves, further, that critical portions of a great many rites are composed of verbal formulas, and these are surely scoreable according to conventional canons of pronunciation applied to alphabetic writing. Analogously, musical components constitutive of rites are scoreable, in a nontrivial way, by one or another method, traditional or modern. As for bodily movement, available notations for the dance are, one would suppose, applicable also to rites. In any case, there is no theoretical bar to increasing notationality for any of these aspects of ritual. Are rites, then, to be judged as uniformly *allographic*? The question requires a consideration of differences between art and ritual, to which we now turn.

5 NOTATION AND NUMBER

Two differences between art and ritual, relative to notation, must be addressed. One concerns the number of items to be identified; the other concerns conditions on the performers. We consider first the question of number. Recall that the drive for notationality in the arts, according to Goodman, is the need for identification of a work from performance to performance. An additional fact about the arts, however, is the continuing stream of new works to be acknowledged, indeed the inexhaustible number of works to be accommodated by an identifying notation. There is, for example, no limit to the number of musical works to be provided for in a notation that accords with antecedent musical practice. And the standard scoring system for music in fact accommodates an infinite number of works.

Rites are in this respect quite different, at least within any given religious or cultural system. For in any such system, the rites to be identified constitute a finite and, typically, a manageably small number. The problem of scoring seems therefore not nearly so severe as in the case of the arts. Not having to devise a "universal" system, that is, one with infinite potential, one may imagine a restricted language yielding for each rite a correlated description, the whole set of such descriptions satisfying notational requirements.[12] With a list of all the regimented rite-descriptions before us, we apply the system by running through the whole list before making any decision. This sort of system seems to me to approximate more closely than the "universal" system of standard musical notation the process of authoritative identification of rituals by their adherents. The matter is of course quite different if we think not of adherents but of anthropologists, whose concern is identifying rites cross-culturally and, indeed, in a potentially universal manner. This concern does seek a scoring system with infinite potential, like that of standard musical notation.

6 CONDITIONS ON THE PERFORMER

Let us consider now the second difference between art and ritual, that concerning conditions on the performer. Recall that allographic art, for Goodman, rests on a distinction between constitutive and contingent features of a work, independent of history of production, the constitutive features being singled out by a notation. It is the availability of such a notation that renders forgery of a *work* vacuous. For forgery is deception as to the circumstances of production, and such deception is powerless to alter identification of the performance as belonging to a given work, decidable solely by reference to the score in question. Yet forgery *of a performance* is still possible for an allographic work since it is still possible to deceive as to whether a given performance has certain historical properties – that is, whether or not it is the premiere performance – as distinct from whether it is a sample of the work.

Now a ritual normally imposes constitutive constraints on its performers as well as on its performances. The performers need to be the prescribed ones, the duly constituted, elected, anointed,

12 Syntactic requirements could clearly be satisfied. But even crucial semantic requirements could be met. That is, (1) the class of performances answering to a given rite-description would share no common members with the class associated with any other, and (2) the determination, of any performance not satisfying both of two descriptions, that it does not satisfy the one or the other would be theoretically possible.

or appointed ones, those satisfying the authoritative specifications. A performance of a rite falsely purporting to satisfy such constraints will in fact be a forgery not merely of a given performance but of the rite itself. While an orchestral performance conforming exactly to the score of a given symphony will be an instance of that symphonic work no matter who the players may be, a ritual performance that exactly obeys the prescribed specifications will, typically, not be an instance of the rite if the performers do not themselves satisfy additional constraints. Such constraints may, for example, characterize legitimate performers in terms of a chain of transfers of authority leading back to particular origins, thus hinging authentication of the rite on history of production and rendering it autographic as a consequence.

Gareth Matthews, emphasizing this point, adduces the Christian Mass as an example, requiring the celebrant to be a priest ordained by a bishop standing in the Apostolic Succession – that is, a bishop ordained by a bishop, ordained by a bishop . . . ordained by one of the Apostles. A feature of the history of production is here constitutive of the rite. Thus, deception as to possession of this feature by a given performance that is otherwise adequate forges the rite itself – which is, accordingly, to be judged autographic rather than allographic.[13]

Taking the impossibility of forging a work as the criterion of its allographic character, are we not driven to conclude that ritual is, generally speaking, not allographic – at least in every case in which constitutive conditions are imposed on performers? Since every such case requires us to ask, "By whom was the rite performed?" do we not necessarily appeal to history of production, so acknowledging the rite as autographic? I think the general conclusion does not follow. For the question, "By whom was the rite performed?" can be given more than one interpretation.

Goodman writes,

Where there is a theoretically decisive test for determining that an object has all the constitutive properties of the work in ques-

13 Gareth Matthews, "Comments on Israel Scheffler," *Synthese*, 46 (March 1981), 439–44.

tion without determining how or by whom the object was produced, there is no requisite history of production and hence no forgery of any given work.[14]

But the phrase "by whom the object was produced" covers two sorts of cases – one, where there is no distinction, independent of history of production, between constitutive and contingent properties of the producers themselves, and the other, where there is. It is the first case alone that Goodman has in mind, and he illustrates it as follows, "The only way of ascertaining that the *Lucretia* before us is genuine is thus to establish the historical fact that it is the actual object made by Rembrandt."[15] Being Rembrandt is the crucial productive property here, and it is not further analyzed into constitutive features shareable by persons other than Rembrandt. Hence, deception as to the property for a given painting constitutes forgery of the work, and the question, "By whom was the painting produced?" asks, "By Rembrandt or by anyone else?"

But the case of ritual is, at least sometimes, different. The constraints on performers of a rite may indeed comprise conditions beyond the performance that forms its focus. But what such constraints may require of the performers are prior or additional performances also scoreable independently of history of production. They may, for example, require that performers carry out a preliminary cleansing by stipulated methods, or undergo a prior or concurrent period of silence or fasting, or undertake any of an indefinitely large array of other auxiliary procedures. A successful performance of the rite as a whole will thus be identifiable by a score referring not only to constitutive features of the focal performance alone, but also to constitutive features of the performers as well – that is, to their having properly executed preparatory or auxiliary requirements. "By whom was the rite performed?" does not here mean "By John Doe or by anyone else?" but rather "By persons satisfying the entire set of specifications or not?" And if the score has been satisfied as a whole, no deception as to further

14 Goodman, *Languages of Art*, p. 122.
15 Ibid., p. 116.

circumstances of production or the identity of the producers will constitute a forgery of the rite as distinct from the particular performance.

Of course, just as the fourth movement of a Brahms symphony, itself allographic, may have a performance that falsely purports to have been preceded by a performance of the previous three, so the focal segment of a rite, itself allographic, may have a performance that falsely purports to have been preceded by performance of its constitutive preparatory procedures. But such forgery of the particular performance is to be distinguished from forgery of the symphony or of the rite itself. Identity of the rite, as of its focal part alone, is determined (just as is the symphony and its fourth movement alone) wholly by conformity with the relevant score, independently of the history of production. Rites of the sort just considered, inclusive of constitutive conditions on their performers, thus turn out allographic after all.

The question of the intent of performers may be raised as an independent threat to the allographic character of ritual. For if, as may be suggested, certain rites require not merely a pattern of performance but also a specific intent on the part of performers, notationality is precluded since the evaluation of intent is notoriously difficult. Now, in any case rites do not uniformly require intent. Moreover, even where a given rite is in fact thought to require intent, we must ask what the force of the requirement is: Does its violation void the rite or merely diminish its value, rendering it, in Austin's terminology, hollow?[16] Finally, let us suppose a given rite indeed requires intent for its identification and not merely its merit. There is here no theoretical obstacle to notationality. For notationality in itself does not presuppose ease of application; it is therefore not precluded by difficulty. If it is at least theoretically possible to tell whether a relevant intent has been achieved, the notational system may incorporate features of intent along with other constitutive features.

16 J. L. Austin, *How to Do Things with Words* (Cambridge, Mass: Harvard University Press, 1962), p. 16.

7 RITUAL AND EXPRESSION

A rite may not only literally exemplify certain features, but also metaphorically exemplify. In this way it enters the domain of expression, in the sense elaborated in Goodman's theory. A feature expressed by a symbol is metaphorically exemplified by it, that is, possessed by it metaphorically as well as referred to by it (although the converse does not hold). For the theory in question, a rite (or its typical performance) may accordingly express a wide range of properties, that is, be denoted metaphorically by a wide range of terms to which it also makes reference. A ritual may thus, for example, express joy or sorrow, humility, yearning, contrition, triumph, grief, trust, steadfastness, elation, exaltation, supplication, gratitude.

The multiply symbolic character of ritual should here be recalled. Expression is not a matter of what the symbol denotes or characterizes, but of what denotes or characterizes it. The expressive reference made by the symbol is that of exemplification, not denotation. And whatever a given rite may in fact portray, it may simultaneously exemplify, literally or metaphorically, quite different things. Explicitly representing episodes of a sacred story, it may at the same time express, rather than represent, dependence or victory, atonement, or thirst for redemption.

Now for this theory of expression, the expression of a feature by a symbol is not to be identified with the having of it by the user or viewer. "The properties a symbol expresses are its own property," writes Goodman. "That the actor was despondent, the artist high, the spectator gloomy or nostalgic or euphoric, the subject inanimate, does not determine whether the face or picture is sad or not. The cheering face of the hypocrite expresses solicitude, and the stolid painter's picture of boulders may express agitation."[17] In the same way, the feelings, thoughts, or other mental states of performers or spectators of a rite are to be distinguished from the features expressed by the rite itself – at least under the present interpretation of expression.

17 Goodman, *Languages of Art*, pp. 85–6.

Yet ritual seems to present a radically different aspect. For rituals are, in religious as distinct from magical contexts, typically intended to penetrate to the heart. Performers of rites are not actors. Although both actors and performers of religious ritual may indeed execute their respective performances flawlessly while their thoughts or feelings are far from the features expressed, a major point of ritual though not of drama, is to affect thoughts and feelings, in part through exposure to such features. Unlike a dramatic performance, a religious ritual usually has a characteristic pattern of recurrence; it is to be repeated with the seasons or with other units of time, or with important junctures of a life. Such regular recurrence is intended to pattern the sensibilities of adherents, in good part by repeated contact with features exemplified and expressed.

True, not every expressed feature is, even theoretically, to be paralleled in the participant, in ritual as in art: For example, a rite expressing majesty may rather be hoped to induce faith or trust. And even where parallel features are indeed hoped for, successful execution of a rite on any given occasion does not hinge on satisfaction of this hope; that a participant's state of mind is incongruous with the expressed theme of the rite may lower its quality but does not, in general, argue that the rite has not taken place. Yet there is, in the case of ritual, a certain linkage between expressed properties and participants' mentality and sensibility; the cognition of expressed features, reinforced by repeated performance, is a major medium of such linkage. While in painting or drama, the cheering face of the hypocrite may, as Goodman says, express solicitude, hypocrisy being irrelevant, it is absurd to suppose that hypocrisy is irrelevant to the performance of a religious rite expressive, say, of contrition or repentance. While in both cases hypocrisy is independent of what is expressed by the performance, it is only in the ritual case relevant to understanding the whole pattern of associated performances, intended, as it is, to reduce hypocrisy in the participants themselves.[18]

18 For a recent study of the relation of ritual to feeling, see Gareth Matthews, "Ritual and the Religious Feelings," in Amelie O. Rorty, ed., *Explaining Emotions* (Berkeley: University of California Press, 1980), pp. 339–53.

8 THE PROBLEM OF MIMETIC
IDENTIFICATION

Mimetic ritual poses a difficult problem of interpretation in those cases where mimicry seems to pass over into identification. A consideration of this problem will lead us to the study of a further symbolic mode beyond those already distinguished. I introduce the problem in the context of an example from the ancient Near East.

Thorkild Jacobsen describes a cult festival of the end of the third millenium in the city of Isin, then the ruling city of Southern Mesopotamia. Annually, the marriage of the goddess Inanna to the god Dumuzi was celebrated, in a rite in which a priestess and the human king not only took on these respective roles but were *identified* with Inanna and Dumuzi. "Why," asks Jacobsen, "should . . . the human ruler and . . . a priestess transcend their human status, take on the identities of the deities Dumuzi and Inanna, and go through their marriage?" In answer to this question, he appeals to what he describes as a

> tenet of mythopoeic logic that similarity and identity merge; "to be like" is as good as "to be". Therefore, by being like, by enacting the role of, a force in nature, a god, man could in the cult enter into and clothe himself with the identity of these powers, with the identity of the gods, and through his own actions, when thus identified, cause the powers involved to act as he would have them act. By identifying himself with Dumuzi, the king is Dumuzi; and similarly the priestess is Inanna – our texts clearly state this.

The phenomenon of identification is one that, according to Jacobsen, recurs in major rites of other sorts as well.[19]

Yet the interpretation proposed by Jacobsen is not persuasive, in that it presupposes mimicry to rest upon similarity. But while miming may indeed exemplify certain movements involved in

19 Thorkild Jacobsen, chap. 5, "Mesopotamia," in H. Frankfort, H. A. Frankfort, John A. Wilson, and Thorkild Jacobsen, *Before Philosophy* (Baltimore: Penguin Books, 1946), pp. 214–15.

the activity being represented, it does not follow that what the mime is doing is *similar* to what he is representing. Nor does it follow that a 3" × 5" snapshot of the Grand Canyon, exemplifying many of its hues, is therefore *similar* to the Grand Canyon. What, anyhow, could be meant by saying, as Jacobsen does, that a man was *like* a force in nature? Representation or denotation needs in general to be distinguished from similarity, and the distinction is particularly important for mimicry, in which certain features of the thing denoted may also be exemplified by the miming action.

If appeal to similarity is, however, to be surrendered in interpreting mimetic identification, how, alternatively, is this phenomenon to be understood? Let us start from the fact that the mime or the miming is to be considered a representing or denotative symbol. The transition to be explained is one that begins with this fact and ends with taking the mime or the miming to be itself what is represented or denoted.

Some theorists have in fact left the matter thus, in effect promoting the transition itself into a principle of explanation free of all reference to similarity. The new principle becomes "the coalescence of a symbol and the thing it stands for," in the formulation of H. Frankfurt and H. A. Frankfort, who offer as an example "the treating of a person's name as an essential part of him – as if it were, in a way, identical with him."[20] This alternative is, however, also unsatisfying. For if the passage from mimicry to identification wants explanation, the general transition from symbol to thing is even more puzzling. The similarity theory at least recognized the need for an intermediary notion to ease the transition from the mime to the mimed. The present theory, offering no intermediary notion at all, generalizes, rather, the problematic transition into one that characterizes not only mimetic but all denoting symbols. Since, moreover, this generalized transition remains opaque, the theory is strongly motivated to postulate a radical and unhappy confusion peculiar to the ancient mind. "For us," say H. Frankfurt and H. A. Frankfort, "there is an essential

---

20 H. Frankfurt et al., *Before Philosophy*, p. 21. See also Ernst Cassirer, *Language and Myth* (New York: Dover [copyright 1946 by Harper and Brothers]), chap. 4, esp. p. 49.

difference between an act and a ritual or symbolical performance."[21] We, but presumably not the ancients, can tell the difference between a symbol and what it stands for – between a horse and the spoken word "horse," between a picture of a lion and the real thing, between rain and the mere promise of rain.

The problem is indeed to understand the psychological transition between a symbol of something and the thing symbolized, but what is needed for such understanding is some additional idea capable of mediating the transition. This idea should, preferably, also be free of appeal to similarity and should postulate no radical difference between the ancient and the modern mind.

9 RITUAL AND MENTION-SELECTION

I have suggested that mention-selection may serve the purpose here. Denotative and mention-selective habits are, as I have suggested, closely related in the development and deployment of terms. That the same term refers *denotatively* to a given object and *mention-selectively* to itself, as well as parallel representations of the object, thus gives a foothold to the transition we have been seeking. For in the very learning of the term itself, it has the double function of denotation and of selecting its parallel mentions as well. And the confusion of these two legitimate functions of the same word, whether by children or adults, ancient or modern, seems more understandable than the bare confusion of a symbol, considered solely as denoting, with its denotatum.[22]

This suggestion yields, at any rate, the following interpretation of mimetic ritual: The mimetic gesture portraying the act of a god is in such capacity denotative. In addition, however, it mention-selects representations of the same act, itself included. But then, by confusion of such mention-selection with denotation, the gesture in question is itself taken to be the act of a god, and not merely the portrayal of such act.

Analogous remarks might also be made about the mechanism by which sacred objects employed in ritual are regarded not

21 Ibid., p. 22.
22 See Chapter 1 and 2, this volume.

merely as symbolic but, in Langer's words, "as life-givers and death dealers, . . . not only revered, but also besought, trusted, feared, placated with service and sacrifice."[23] The fierce biblical polemic against idol worship makes it very difficult to fathom the mentality of those who would attribute powers of life and death to mere sticks and stones; indeed, the polemic is *intended* to ridicule such mentality. Cannot "idol worshippers" see that their graven images are merely inert and powerless things? "Their idols are silver and gold, the work of men's hands. They have mouths, but they speak not; Eyes have they but they see not, etc."[24] Several modern scholars have given a more sympathetic interpretation to idol worship, so-called. Indeed, it was not the images themselves that were worshipped, they say, but the gods or forces symbolized by these images. Such a view gives a more favorable view of so-called idol worship. However, in recognizing only the denotative mode of reference, it gives little basis for grasping the genuine phenomenon of identification we have discussed or the causal efficacy ascribed to sacred symbols, noted in the preceding quotation from Langer. Even the Bible suggests such causal efficacy, if not for images of the deity, then for other sacred objects. As Langer notes, "The sacred ark going up before the children of Israel gives them their victory. Held by the Philistines, it visits disease on its captors. Its efficacy is seen in every triumph of the community, every attainment and conquest."[25] My suggestion of mention-selection as an additional symbolic

---

23 Susanne K. Langer, *Philosophy in a New Key* (New York: Penguin Books, 1942, 1948), p. 124.
24 Psalm 115. On the biblical polemic against idolatry, see the brilliant interpretation of Yehezkel Kaufmann, *The Religion of Israel* (Chicago: University of Chicago Press, 1960), pp. 13ff., 19–20, 146, 236–7, 387. It is interesting that Kaufmann writes, "[Israelite religion] rejected representations of God because such images were regarded in paganism as an embodiment of the gods and, as such, objects of a cult" (p. 237). It is also interesting, relative to the phenomenon of identification we have discussed, to note Kaufmann's comment on prophetic universalism, referring particularly to Isaiah 2: "Idolatry is conceived of as arising out of human pride. . . . Trusting in his power [man] makes himself gods; in adoring them, he worships himself" (p. 387).
25 Langer, *Philosophy in a New Key*, p. 125. (See also, e.g., 1 Samuel 5).

function beyond denotation is intended also to make such phenomena more understandable.

10 COMMEMORATIVE RITUAL

Many religious rituals center on particular events in sacred story. I call these "commemorative rituals." The connection between rite and myth, between celebration and story, is indeed so close that it is for the most part exceedingly difficult to disentangle origins. Whether, as some suppose, rite initially derived from myth or whether, as others think, myth originated in rite is a matter we need not try to decide. What is clear is that there are at present intimate connections between rite and story and that, in major cases of religious ritual, the stories are not *mere* stories but rather are believed to relate true and momentous historical occurrences.

I distinguish two different relations in connection with commemorative rituals, that between the designated historical event and the ritual act celebrating it, and that between one such ritual act and its parallel ritual acts, whenever or by whomever they are performed. The first relation is of a denotative sort; that is, the ritual act portrays or represents the historical event.[26] The second relation holds between performances of the same ritual; it relates ritual equivalents or replicas.

These relations are clearly different. That two performances are ritual equivalents does not imply that there is some one historical event that they denote in common. They may denote something else than a historical event; they may both have null denotation; or they may not purport to denote at all, lacking even null denotation. And that a ritual act denotes a particular historical act clearly does not imply that they are ritual equivalents, even though the former may exemplify certain features of the latter. The historical event is in general not itself a rite; moreover, it is typically denoted or portrayed rather than replicated in ritual, just as the

---

26 For brevity's sake, I do not here treat cases of null denotation, that is, cases where there was no event of the sort purportedly represented in the ritual act in question. Such cases would need to be treated nonrelationally, as involving certain historical event symbols of denotative kind but with null denotation.

mimed activity is in general portrayed rather than replicated or exemplified by the mime.

11 RITUAL AND REENACTMENT

This suggests caution in applying the concept of reenactment even to the interpretation of commemorative rituals, let alone others. Even where the explicit intent of a rite is to encourage an empathic and spiritual union with the historical actors in question, it does not follow that the rite replicates the activities of these actors. The ritual in one or another way may rather portray the designated event, relating it in story, exemplifying certain of its ingredient features, or expressing related feelings, all intended to promote empathic union. Nevertheless, such intended union is to be distinguished from literal reenactment or replication.

In the Jewish Seder feast celebrating the Exodus from Egypt, the Haggadah text is recited, one passage of which reads, "In every generation one ought to regard oneself as though he had personally come out of Egypt."[27] The whole Seder ritual is intended to foster spiritual identification with the liberated Israelites of the Exodus and to kindle in participants a vivid sense of the joy of redemption from slavery. But the various symbolic means through which the ritual strives to accomplish this goal do not add up to a literal reenactment of the portrayed historical Exodus. Rather, the story of the Exodus is described, elaborated, and emphasized – the Exodus portrayed as a key event in history. The empathic identification sought is intended not only to lay down a particular past event as a major temporal marker, but to make that event come alive now, that is, to bring some of its main features into the temporal foreground. It is in order to promote the contemporary appreciation of freedom that the Haggadah declares, "Not only our forefathers did the Holy One, Blessed be He, redeem, but also ourselves did He redeem with them."[28] The

27 Passover Haggadah, numerous editions. For a general account see Theodore H. Gaster, *Festivals of the Jewish Year* (New York: Sloane, 1952, 1953).
28 Ibid. My point in this paragraph disagrees with the position of Gaster, who apparently takes the view that the goal of personal identification is associated

actions comprising the ritual nevertheless do not reenact, but rather portray the historical redemption celebrated.

On the other hand, the notion of reenactment may appropriately describe the relation of a ritual performance to its past replicas. For each such performance refers indirectly to such past replicas, that is, alludes to them, while independently denoting whatever it may denote and symbolizing in the other modes so far distinguished. In the regular recurrence of a given rite, a sense builds up, in each new performance, of the prior performances that have taken place through the lifetime of the participants but, normally, beyond these as well, to the time of the ritual's origin nearest the commemorated historical event.

In such allusion, we have, I suggest, a further symbolic mode. The mode of reference involved here is neither denotation, nor exemplification, nor expression, nor mention-selection. The relation of one performance to a replica is a relation holding between performances denoted by and exemplifying the same ritual specifications. These performances are, so to speak, on the same symbolic level. If we picture denotation as running downward from symbol to object, then exemplification and expression will run upward from denoted object to (certain) symbols. Mention-selection, in this picture, will run laterally from symbol to parallel symbols. And the replica relation involved in reenactment will also run laterally, from object to parallel objects, that is, from performances to others of the same kind.

Such referential replication may be explained as reference transmitted through a chain composed of symbolic links already distinguished. A given performance is linked to the ritual specification that it exemplifies. The specification in question is in turn linked to other (past) performances exemplifying it. The allusion

with reenactment of the historical event commemorated. He writes that "when the Jew recites [the Haggadah], he is performing an act not of remembrance but of personal identification in the here and now" (ibid., p. 42), and he writes also, "Those present at the Seder ceremony are expected to adopt a casual, reclining posture, symbolizing that of freemen at ancient banquets. In some parts of the world, however, everyone appears in hat and coat, with satchel on back and staff in hand, thus *re-enacting* the Departure from Egypt" (p. 40, my italics).

by the first performance to the rest thus may be thought of as transmitted through a two-link chain of exemplification.[29]

While such chains, of varying length and complexity, are theoretically available everywhere, they become referentially operative in only certain, and not other, cases – or at least not other cases to the same degree. Thus, the notion of reenactment plays no role, or virtually no role, in the arts, at least by comparison with religious ritual. A given performance of a musical work makes no reference to past performances of the same work any more than it denotes a significant historical event.[30] By contrast, a ritual performance, I suggest, alludes to its own past kin, just as it may point back to a commemorated event. The sense of reenacting, reexperiencing, an important procedure is strong here: The relevant chain is referentially activated, and it is perhaps a likely symptom of the religious consciousness that it is thus activated.

Such activation gives some body to the notion of tradition, so strong in religious contexts. A tradition is not merely a repeated sequence of acts; any set of nonsimultaneous acts forms a repeated sequence of *some* sort. Even, however, when allowable sorts are somehow restricted, mere mindless repetition makes no tradition. What is needed is some sense of the fact, with each repetition, that it *is* a repetition, that is, some sense of its predecessors. And that may perhaps be interpretable, according to my proposal, as the reference, via a chain running through commonly exemplified specifications, by each act to its relevant predecessors.

The marking out of important historical events defining a temporal matrix, and the concomitant reenactive reference to a ritual tradition, serves also to form a conception of community. For the performers of past ritual replicas constitute a body of actors to which present performers severally relate themselves through the reenactment in question, and hence, indirectly, to one another contemporaneously. The community thus defined, bears, like all

---

29 The concept of chains of reference has been noted in Goodman, *Languages of Art*, p. 92, and elaborated in Goodman, "Routes of Reference," Second Congress of International Association for Semiotic Studies, Vienna, 1979.

30 For discussion of a different form of musical reference, see V. A. Howard, "On Musical Quotation," *Monist*, 58 (1974), 307–18.

communities, not only certain common bonds to the past, but also certain common orientations in the present. In sum, an organization of time, as well as of the space occupied by a historical community, is facilitated.

Since the previous discussion has relied largely on religious and ancient example, I close with a contemporary and secular illustration. Speaking of Parliament, a recent English writer remarks:

> There are many whose cynicism . . . has been tempered by participating in some of the majesty of its rituals, most of which are steeped in historical significance. Such rituals help to unite the past with the future and to convey the sense of participation in a shared form of life. They do something to mitigate the feeling any rational being must have about the triviality and transience of his life upon earth. They do much, too, to develop that feeling of fraternity which is the life-blood of any effective institution.[31]

31 R. S. Peters, *Ethics and Education* (London: Allen & Unwin, 1966, 1970), pp. 318–19.

Chapter 11
Ritual change

When does a change *in* a rite become a change *of* the rite? The answer depends, obviously, on how the rite is individuated. But that is only the beginning of the story.

Rites are multiple rather than singular symbolic entities.[1] That is, rites are identified by practice not with single performances, but rather with groups of performances satisfying certain specifications. In this respect, they resemble musical works and etchings, rather than paintings. How are ritual specifications formulated? There is variation, of course. They may be passed on by oral tradition, or written down, or may only be tacit though well understood in context. But in every case they lay down conditions that must be satisfied, defining a right way and a wrong way of doing things if the rite is to be realized.

1 AUTOGRAPHIC AND ALLOGRAPHIC RITES

Theoretically, rites may be *autographic* or *allographic*, in Nelson Goodman's terminology, depending on whether the ritual identity of their associated performances depends on the history of

"Ritual Change" appeared in *Revue Internationale de Philosophie*, 46, no. 185 (1993), 151–60.

1 On singular and multiple arts, see Nelson Goodman, *Languages of Art* (Indianapolis, Ind.: Hackett, 1976), p. 115.

their production.[2] Just as etchings are autographic in that the work identity of their associated prints consists in their common source in an original plate, so rites are autographic when the ritual identity of their associated performances depends on the linkage of their performers to a common chain of historic authorizations.[3] Rites whose identities are not thus, or otherwise, dependent upon the historical character of their associated performances are allographic. In either case, specifications of a rite define conditions that must be met for a performance to qualify as an instance of the rite at all.

2 FORMALITY AND RIGIDITY OF RITES

Many writers have emphasized the rigidity of ritual, its formalized and relentless fixity – hence its contrast with an intelligent fitting of means to ends in pursuit of a purpose, under conditions of contextual variation. Ernst Cassirer's description of sacrificial services may serve as one example representing innumerable others making the same point. "The . . . service is fixed by very definite objective rules, a set sequence of words and acts which must be carefully observed if the sacrifice is not to fail in its purpose."[4] And again:

> From the point of view of primitive thought the slightest alteration in the established scheme of things is disastrous. The words of a magic formula, of a spell or incantation, the single phases of a religious act, of a sacrifice or prayer, all this must be repeated in one and the same invariable order. Any change would annihilate the force and efficiency of the magical word or religious rite. Primitive religion can therefore leave no room for any freedom of individual thought. It prescribes its fixed,

2 On autographic versus allographic art, see ibid., pp. 113ff.
3 On this question, see Gareth Matthews, "Comments on Israel Scheffler," *Synthese*, 46 (1981), 439–44, and Chapter 10, this volume.
4 Ernst Cassirer, *The Philosophy of Symbolic Forms.* Vol. 2, *Mythical Thought* (New Haven, Conn.: Yale University Press, 1955), p. 221.

rigid, inviolable rules not only for every human action but also for every human feeling.[5]

It is important, however, to distinguish the question of ritual identity from that of rigidity. Identity is a matter of definitive specification of the rite itself; rigidity concerns rather the attitude taken toward the rite as defined – fanatical adherence in the belief as to what Cassirer refers to as its "force and efficiency," and the "disastrous" character of any "alteration in the established scheme of things" – particularly, the failure to perform the rite when required by the cult. It is especially important to separate the formality of a ritual – what Cassirer describes as "its formalized and relentless fixity" – from the attitude of compulsive adherence to its performance. A Mozart piano concerto is as formally constituted as any rite, but to speak of its rigidity is absurd. The score prescribes what sequence of notes is to be taken as constitutive of the work; it does not also prescribe that the work so constituted be performed. Similarly the definition of a rite prescribes *what* performances are to be taken as individuating the rite; it does not also prescribe *that* the rite be performed.

3 THE BIRTH AND DEATH OF RITES

No doubt rites, definitively constituted as they are, have histories. Often, they have crystallized out of events or practices lacking such definitive character, their specifications as yet unformed. Without such specifications, a practice is fluid, its identity conditions not fixed; "same rite" and "different rite" are as yet unclear.

When such a fluid practice crystallizes sufficiently to articulate defining specifications, ritual identity is assured. Such change is, however, neither change in a rite nor change of a rite, for there was here no rite to begin with. Rather it represents the origination of a ritual category where there was none before – the birth of a rite, so to speak. Conversely, we may speak of the dissolution of a ritual category when its specifications loosen or weaken; here, so to speak, is the death of a rite. Secularization of religious rites is

5 Ernst Cassirer, *An Essay on Man* (New Haven, Conn.: Yale University Press, 1944), p. 225.

often not a matter of simple nonperformance but involves a gradual attenuation of ritual identities, a blurring of heretofore definitive boundaries, so that it becomes unclear when a performance of the rite has taken place. Such dissolution is characterizable only by extreme understatement as change in a rite; so might a man's death be described as a change in him. Nor is there, in the notion of a rite's dissolution, any suggestion of a replacement, for example, of change of one rite for another.

4 FREQUENCY OF OBSERVANCE

Aside from the birth and death of rites, that is, the origination of ritual categories and their dissolution, we may of course also recognize changes in the prevalence of ritual performances clearly assignable to such categories. The frequency of ritual observance of course waxes and wanes independently of the mere availability of definitive ritual specifications. But such alteration of frequency is no more a change *in,* nor a change *of,* the rite than alteration in the frequency of a concerto's performance constitutes revision of the concerto. Assuming now that we set aside processes of origination and dissolution of ritual categories, as well as alterations in the frequency of ritual observances, what other sorts of ritual change can be envisaged?

5 CHANGE IN MODE OF PERFORMANCE

To begin with, there may be a change in the mode of performance of a rite that does not violate the ritual specifications in force. The new mode may be utterly novel; alternatively it may on occasion have occurred earlier but only now become so frequent as to be familiar or even prevalent. Such a change, compatible with ruling specifications, is clearly not a change of the rite, but rather a change in the rite. The rite, identified by its unchanged specifications, has not itself undergone alteration, and a new performance in the old style will still qualify as an instance of the rite in question.

6 NEW RITUAL SPECIFICATIONS

Furthermore, there is the growth or promulgation of a new set of specifications to replace the old. Here we evidently have the change of a rite. What, however, can be meant by replacement? When we have two different sets of performance specifications, we have in fact just two discrete ritual categories – two nonidentical rites. The question of replacement goes beyond the issue of mere identity, appealing to some criterion for selecting among nonidentical rites.

The role or function of a rite typically serves as such a criterion and is normally indicated by the way the rite is named. Thus, the marriage rite is the rite that *has the function* of effecting the marriage relation of two persons. To say that one rite replaces another *as* the marriage rite is then to say that one set of ritual specifications newly assumes the role or function of another set in effecting the marriage relation. We have exchanged one rite for another as the means of initiating marriage. Once the replacement has been made, a performance satisfying the earlier specifications will no longer count as an instance of the *marriage* rite, that is, as an instance of the rite having the function of initiating marriage. Nor would a performance satisfying the new specifications have counted earlier as an instance of the marriage rite.

7 SPECIFICATION BY PERFORMANCE AND BY FUNCTION

It is important to note that reference to a rite by definitive specifications differs from reference to that rite by role or function. Change *of* a rite may, as we have argued, be understood as replacement of one rite, definitively specified by performance, by another rite, so specified, for effecting a given function. But the same process of replacement may be described as a change *in* the marriage rite, that is, a change in the ritual way the function of marriage is effected. With ritual specification by function alone, there has been a change only in the means of implementation. With ritual definitively specified by performance, however, there has been replacement of one rite by another.

Specification by function lends itself to a certain ambiguity. "The marriage rite" thus refers to one or another of several nonidentical rites having the same function at different times. Context typically resolves such ambiguity, but an explicit time reference may be invoked, where necessary, to settle any lingering doubt, for example, "the marriage rite in the fourth century."

8 SPECIFICATION BY AUTHORITY

As well, the definitive specification of a rite may hinge on the ruling of a relevant authority at a given time. That is to say, differing performances may all comply with a decisive superordinate specification referring to authoritative decision. The superordinate specification says, in effect, that the rite in question is to be performed at a given time exactly as the authority at that time requires it to be performed.

Assume that the authority's subordinate specification for a given rite at a certain time differs from its subordinate specification at a later time. Is a performance at the earlier time, which complies with the earlier specification, an instance of the rite – and indeed the same rite – as a performance at the later time complying with the later specification? Conversely, does a performance at the later time, which complies with the earlier specification, or a performance at the earlier time complying with the later specification invariably fail to qualify as an instance of the rite in question? To say yes to both these questions is to say that neither subordinate specification alone lays down a conclusive condition for belonging to the rite in question. Neither condition alone is either necessary or sufficient for such belonging. It is only the superordinate specification relativizing every explicit authoritative specification to time that provides a necessary and sufficient condition for ritual identity. Here we have, then, no change *of* the rite, which remains the same before and after the critical time in question, but we do have a change in the rite.

Since we have no change of the rite, this case differs from that previously considered, in which the name of rites by function alone lends itself to ambiguity in applying to nonidentical rites. "The civil marriage rite," naming the rite by reference to institutional authority, skirts the ambiguity in question. The notion of a ritual replica is, here, from the point of view of performance alone, wider than that applying in the previous case, since it crosses the boundary of the change from one subordinate performance specification to another. Another implication is that the notion of reenactment, in which each ritual performance refers to all previous replicas,[6] is analogously expanded to embrace whatever performances may have been prescribed by the authority in question, no matter how variable in other respects.

It is worth noting that the specification of a ritual by reference to the rulings of an institutional authority differs from other forms of symbolic specification. Imagine defining a symphony as whatever class of musical performances accords with the rulings of some authority on the days of the performances in question. Such a definition would, among other things, render the symphony autographic, since its identity would hinge on the historical facts pertaining to the rulings of the authority in question. Similarly, rites defined by reference to authoritative rulings are rendered autographic; their identities are not abstracted from the question of their historical origins.

9 SEMANTIC CHANGE

Consider now the case of semantic change of a rite, that is, the alteration not of its constitutive performances but of their references, whether denotative or exemplificational or expressive. The characteristic gestures, let us imagine, remain unchanged, but what they refer to now differs from what went before. Do we have here change in a rite or change of a rite? To say it is change of a rite is to overestimate by far the number of rites, supposing a new rite for every referential nuance. It seems also to overlook the fact that every rite carries different interpretations. On the other hand, to say it is merely change in a rite drives us to rule that two ritual gestures in different cultures, which happen to be coincidentally the same but are referentially divergent, constitute the selfsame rite.

6 On my notion of reenactment, see Chapter 10, this volume.

Perhaps, it may be suggested, we need to recognize the factor of relevant culture, or community, explicitly. Accordingly, referential differences associated with the same gestures in a given cultural system would be reckoned compatible with ritual identity, while such differences attached to identical gestures in different systems would be deemed incompatible with ritual identity. A difficulty with this proposal is its appeal to the notion of a cultural system, which lacks clear criteria of individuation.

10 EXEMPLIFICATION

A more likely proposal is to require of ritual replicas that they exemplify, that is to say, both satisfy and refer to the same specifications.[7] Similarity of gesture alone is, according to this proposal, powerless to guarantee replicahood; the critical issue in whether a given gesture refers to certain specifications that it also satisfies, or not. This criterion is sharper than one that depends on the notion of a cultural system; yet it seems effective in ruling out troublesome coincidences of the sort we have considered. That is, coincidentally identical gestures in different cultures are overwhelmingly unlikely to refer to the same specifications even if satisfying them; thus, they would be judged to diverge in their ritual identity. On the other hand, true ritual replicas, coexemplifying the same specifications, could well diverge referentially in every other way.

11 REENACTMENT AND COMMUNITY

The range of reenactment, as already remarked, depends on ritual replicahood, each ritual performance reenacting all those prior performances that it replicates. And replicahood in turn depends, as lately proposed, on coexemplification of the same specifications, irrespective of other referential changes. Thus, ritual replicas may accommodate a wide variety of referential divergences without affecting reenactment. The upshot is that referential change across ritual replicas, such as often occurs in the history of religions, is compatible with identity of the religious community

7 On exemplification, see Goodman, *Languages of Art*, pp. 52ff.

characterized by common reenactments. Indeed, such reenactments serve to define and to strengthen the community, preserving its continuity despite considerable variation among its ritual references.

By contrast, where the coexemplification of ritual specifications is lacking, replicahood fails and, with it, reenactment also, no matter how similar ritual performances may be to one another. Community is here divided; reenactment cannot bridge the gap. A ritual may occasionally *appear* to travel from one community to another, failing, however, to cross the divide between them. In fact, however, it is not the same ritual at the beginning and the end of the journey. Religions in this way often borrow externals from one another. For no matter how alike ritual gestures may be, when reenactment fails to cross the line, each performance is understood as exemplifying the specifications within its own sphere and not those beyond.

12 RITUAL, MUSIC, AND EDUCATION

I have emphasized the importance of exemplification for the identity of rites, hence for reenactment, and for the notion of ritual community, which reenactment enables and reinforces. Such exemplification yields a significant contrast between ritual and music – a contrast that holds despite the fact that both ritual and musical performances are governed by specifications and despite, even, the amenability of ritual performance to scoring – wholly where the rite is allographic and at least partially where conditions on the ritual performers or the institutional definition of the rite render it autographic.[8] In brief, a musical performance complies with its score but does not in general exemplify its score. By contrast, ritual performances not only comply with but also exemplify ritual specifications. Why is compliance alone not sufficient for rites?

We have already seen the importance of exemplification in ruling out troublesome cross-cultural coincidences. But a deeper reason may perhaps be suggested: In many, perhaps most, rites,

8 Regarding ritual and scoring, see Chapter 10, this volume

governing specifications function as the property of the whole community, whereas musical scores do not in the same way function as the property of the whole community. The musical score, that is to say, is essential for the performers to know, but is not essential for the audience to know. It is true that the more the audience knows of the score, the greater is its understanding. Nevertheless, knowledge of the score is not essential to a grasp of the music, nor is the musical performance itself generally considered an educational occasion, initiating the audience into an appreciation of the score. Of course, communities of aspiring musicians need to acquire knowledge of relevant musical specifications. But these students are preparing for careers performing for larger audiences of whom the same is not true. The educational features of the students' own training are not transferred to the wider settings in which they practice their craft.

In contrast to the case of music, the ritual performance typically needs to carry its specifications on its face. That is to say, participants – passive as well as active – need to comprehend the specifications of the actions being carried out. The active performers of course need a surer and more detailed understanding of the specifications that they are responsible for fulfilling; thus priests need to be adept at executing ritual specifications in a way unnecessary to the laity. Yet the laity requires at least a general knowledge of these specifications in order to grasp the point of the performance. In a way unlike that pertaining to music, each ritual performance thus functions also as a demonstration, or teaching act, a purpose of which is to educate the community in the rite's rationale.

Section VI
Symbol and reality

Chapter 12

Science and the world

Science is commonly thought to give us a factual account of reality, a true picture of the world. Yet it consists of alterable hypotheses, perpetually open to change. Unless these hypotheses are somehow, nevertheless, anchored to reality, how can science be deemed to give us true access to the world? A popular response to this problem locates the ultimate authority of science in the given, that is, in what is given with certainty to the senses, leaving all else open to variable interpretation. Yet this response is confused. Error and certainty, like truth and falsehood, are ascribable to descriptions, not, in general, to things described.

1 CERTAINTY AND CONSISTENCY

The so-called certainty of the given cannot protect its purported descriptions from mistake; the given cannot therefore provide a fixed control over conceptualization. If we attempt to picture all our beliefs as somehow controlled by our reports of the given, we shall have to concede that those reports are themselves not rigidly constrained by what is given in fact, since they are themselves subject to error. It does no good, then, to suppose that they constitute points of direct and self-evident contact between our belief systems and reality – firm touchstones by which all our other

"Science and the World" is drawn from my *Science and Subjectivity*, 2nd ed. (Indianapolis, Ind.: Hackett, 1982), Chap. 5.

beliefs are to be judged, but which are themselves beyond criticism. Observation reports, in short, cannot be construed as isolated certainties. They must survive a continuous process of accommodation with our other beliefs, a process in the course of which they may themselves be overridden. The control they exercise lies not in an *infallibility*, which is beyond their reach; it consists rather in an *independence* of other beliefs, an ability to clash with the rest in such a way as to force a systematic review threatening to all.

But can such a conception of independence be sufficient for a theory of objective control over belief? Does it provide an adequate restriction of arbitrariness in the choice of hypotheses? Conflict provides at best, after all, a motivation for restoring consistency. However, if this is the only motivation I am bound to honor, I am free to choose at will among equally coherent bodies of belief at variance with one another; I need not prefer the consistent factual account to the consistent distortion, nor, indeed, to the coherent fairy tale. Faced with a conflict between my observation reports and my theory, I may freely alter or discard the former or the latter or both, as long as I replace my initial inconsistent set of beliefs with one that is coherent. Clearly, this much freedom is too much freedom. Constraints beyond that of consistency must be acknowledged.

Yet in denying the doctrine of certainty, have we not made it impossible to do just that? If all our beliefs are infected with the possibility of error, if none of our descriptions is guaranteed to be true, none can provide us with an absolutely reliable link to reality. Our beliefs float free of fact, and the best we can do is to ensure consistency among them. The dilemma is severe and uncomfortable: Swallow the myth of certainty or concede that we cannot tell fact from fancy.

This dilemma lies at the root of much controversy among scientifically minded philosophers. A review of certain elements of the controversy will enrich our grasp of the problem. I take as the primary object of such review the debate within the Vienna Circle in the 1930s concerning the status of so-called protocol sentences in science. Two chief protagonists in this debate were Otto Neurath and Moritz Schlick, the former rejecting the doctrine of certainty and insisting "that science keeps within the domain of propositions, that propositions are its starting point and terminus,"[1] and the latter urging rather that science is "a means of finding one's way among the facts," its confirmation statements constituting "absolutely fixed points of contact" between "knowledge and reality."[2]

2 NEURATH CONTRA CERTAINTY

I turn first to Neurath, who proposes that scientific operations be understood as wholly confined to the realm of statements:

> It is always science as a system of statements which is at issue. *Statements are compared with statements,* not with "experiences," "the world," or anything else. . . . Each new statement is compared with the totality of existing statements previously coordinated. To say that a statement is correct, therefore, means that it can be incorporated in this totality. What cannot be incorporated is rejected as incorrect. The alternative to rejection of the new statement is, in general, one accepted only with great reluctance: the whole previous system of statements can be modified up to the point where it becomes possible to incorporate the new statement. (SP, p. 291)

Against the notion of a primitive and incorrigible set of so-called protocol statements as the basis of science, Neurath is adamant. "There is no way of taking conclusively established pure protocol sentences as the starting point of the sciences," he

1 Otto Neurath, "Sociology and Physicalism," tr. Morton Magnus and Ralph Raico. Reprinted with permission of The Free Press from *Logical Positivism,* by A. J. Ayer, ed., p. 285. Copyright 1959 by The Free Press, a corporation. Originally appeared as "Soziologie im Physikalismus," *Erkenntnis,* 2 (1931–2). Page references to this article in the text will be preceded by "SP."
2 Moritz Schlick, "The Foundation of Knowledge," tr. David Rynin. Reprinted with permission of The Free Press from *Logical Positivism* by A. J. Ayer, ed., p. 226. Copyright 1959 by The Free Press, a corporation. Originally appeared as "Uber das Fundament der Erkenntnis," *Erkenntnis,* 4 (1934). Page references to Schlick in the text refer to this article.

writes.[3] Aside from tautologies, the protocol as well as the non-protocol sentences of unified science share the same physicalistic form and are subject to the same treatment. The protocol statements are distinguished by the fact that "in them, a personal noun always occurs several times in a specific association with other terms. A complete protocol sentence might, for instance, read: 'Otto's protocol at 3:17 o'clock: [at 3:16 o'clock Otto said to himself: (at 3:15 o'clock there was a table in the room perceived by Otto)]'" (PS, p. 202). However, the main point to be stressed is not that protocol sentences are distinct, but rather that *every law and every physicalistic sentence of unified-science or of one of its sub-sciences is subject to . . . change. And the same holds for protocol sentences*" (PS, p. 203).

The motivation for change is the wish to maintain consistency, for "in unified science we try to construct a non-contradictory system of protocol sentences and non-protocol sentences (including laws). . . . The fate of being discarded may befall even a protocol sentence" (PS, p. 203).

The notion that protocol sentences are primitive and beyond criticism because they are free of interpretation must be abandoned, for "the above formulation of a complete protocol sentence shows that, insofar as personal nouns occur in a protocol, interpretation must *always* already have taken place" (PS, p. 205). Furthermore, there is, within the innermost brackets, an inescapable reference to some person's "act of perception" (PS, p. 205). The conclusion is that no sentence of science is to be regarded as more primitive than any other:

> All are of equal primitiveness. Personal nouns, words denoting perceptions, and other words of little primitiveness occur in all factual sentences. . . . All of which means that *there are neither primitive protocol sentences nor sentences which are not subject to verification.* (PS, p. 205)

3 Otto Neurath, "Protocol Sentences," tr. Frederic Schick. Reprinted with permission of The Free Press from *Logical Positivism* by A. J. Ayer, ed., p. 201. Copyright 1959 by The Free Press, a corporation. Originally appeared as "Protokollsatze," *Erkenntnis*, 3 (1932–3). Page references to this article in the text will be preceded by "PS."

Further, since *"every* language *as such,* is inter-subjective" (PS, 205), it is meaningless to talk of private languages, or to regard protocol languages as initially disparate, requiring ultimately to be brought together in some special manner. On the contrary, "the protocol languages of the Crusoe of yesterday and of the Crusoe of today are as close and as far apart from one another as are the protocol languages of Crusoe and of Friday" (PS, p. 206).

We could conceive of a sorting-machine into which protocol sentences are thrown. The laws and other factual sentences (including protocol sentences) serving to mesh the machine's gears sort the protocol sentences which are thrown into the machine and cause a bell to ring if a contradiction ensues. At this point one must either replace the protocol sentence whose introduction into the machine has led to the contradiction by some other protocol sentence, or rebuild the entire machine. *Who* rebuilds the machine, or *whose* protocol sentences are thrown into the machine is of no consequence whatsoever. (PS, 207)

Neurath stresses the place of prediction in science. Yet, true to his self-imposed restriction to the realm of statements alone, he does not construe the success of a prediction as consisting in its agreement with fact. Rather, he declares, "A prediction is a statement which it is assumed will agree with a future statement" (SP, p. 317).

Despite his refusal, however, to contrast the "thinking personality" with "experience" (SP, p. 290), to compare statements with "'experiences,' 'the world', or anything else" (SP, p. 291), and to ask such "'dangerous' questions . . . as how 'observation' and 'statement' are connected; or, further, how 'sense data' and 'mind', the 'external world' and the 'internal world' are connected,"[4] he slips into what he ought surely to have regarded, in a more careful moment, as dangerous metaphysics:

4 Otto Neurath, *Foundations of the Social Sciences* (Chicago: University of Chicago Press, 1944), p. 5.

Ignoring all meaningless statements, the unified science proper to a given historical period proceeds from proposition to proposition, blending them into a self-consistent system which is an instrument for successful prediction, and, consequently, for life. (SP, p. 286)

To speak rashly in this way of the relation between science and life is clearly to leave the pure realm of statements and to admit, after all, that science cannot be adequately characterized in terms of consistency alone, that its very point, indeed, is to refer to what lies beyond itself.

Surely, not all self-consistent systems are "instruments for life," in the intended sense. He implies that practical usefulness accrues to science in virtue of its yielding successful predictions. However, he understands the success of a prediction to consist simply in its agreement with a later statement; on this criterion all predictions succeed that are followed by reiterations of themselves or by other statements coherent with them.

In the first of the passages by Neurath quoted earlier, he speaks of comparing each new statement with "the totality of existing statements previously coordinated" (SP, p. 291). Perhaps the idea is that there is one presumably coherent totality that is to be singled out as a standard on each occasion of comparison, namely, the totality that was last ratified by acceptance and still in force on that occasion.

However, *acceptance* in itself fails to differentiate between beliefs that are critically accepted on the basis of factual evidence and those that are not. What is of crucial significance, however, is that this method provides no incentive to *revise* the accepted totality of beliefs. For the assumed coherence of this totality can always be preserved by rejecting *all* new conflicting sentences. Neurath concedes that the alternative to such rejection, consisting in revision of the accepted totality, is adopted "only with great reluctance" (SP, p. 291). The mystery, on his account, is why it should ever be adopted at all.

It is, moreover, pertinent to question the assumed interpretation of acceptance: acceptance by whom? The assumption that acceptance singles out one presumably coherent totality on each occasion of comparison is perhaps plausible if we consider just one individual. It is groundless if we take into account the acceptances of the whole "inter-subjective" community in line with Neurath's general attitude. A general appeal to the factor of acceptance yields a multiplicity of conflicting totalities of belief: Which of these is to serve as a standard?

There are passages, indeed, where Neurath makes no appeal to acceptance but acknowledges a plurality of mutually conflicting totalities open to the investigator. To be consistent, the investigator may not choose more than one of these, but there is no further constraint on his or her choice beyond convenience. Thus, Neurath writes:

> A social scientist who, after careful analysis, rejects certain reports and hypotheses, reaches a state, finally, in which he has to face comprehensive sets of statements which compete with other comprehensive sets of statements. All these sets may be composed of statements which seem to him plausible and acceptable. There is no place for an empiricist question: Which is the "true" set? but only whether the social scientist has sufficient time and energy to try more than one set or to decide that he, in regard to his lack of time and energy – and this is the important point – should work with one of these comprehensive sets only.[5]

We find here, to be sure, a passing reference to plausibility and acceptability, but it is wholly unexplained. As to the choice among incompatible systems, any one is as good as any other; only the limitations of time and energy offer a basis for decision. The machine analogy quoted earlier does indeed, as Neurath says, make the point "quite clear." The machine detects contradictions, but aside from a general restriction to physicalistic language, which may be assumed, no principle of selection is supplied for determining its input. Protocol sentences, distinguished solely by their form, may be chosen arbitrarily for insertion. As long as no contradiction has been detected among its virtually arbitrary elements, the machine is to be taken as the very embodiment and

5 Ibid., p. 13.

standard of correctness. The picture is one of unrelieved coherence free of any taint of fact.

What impels Neurath to construct this caricature of science? To appreciate his philosophical motivation is to gain a deeper understanding of the basic dilemma we face between coherence and certainty.

The very notion of an infallible access to fact seems to require the supposition that statement and reality might, through direct comparison, be determined to correspond with each other. But such a supposition is meaningless from Neurath's point of view.

He rejects the philosophical tendency to read linguistic features into reality. The structure of language is not, after all, to be taken naively as a clue to the structure of reality. Facts, in general, understood as peculiar extralinguistic entities precisely parallel to true statements, belong, in Neurath's scheme, to the class of "meaningless duplications . . . to be rejected" (SP, p. 291).[6]

Not only are such duplications superfluous; they mislead us into supposing that in locating them independently and finding them to share the same structure with certain statements, we have a genuine method of justifying the acceptance of these statements. But facts, as entities distinct from the true statements to which they are presumed to correspond, have no careers of their own capable of sustaining such a method. If I am undecided about the truth of the sentence "The car is in the garage," I am equally undecided as to whether or not it is a fact that the car is in the garage: There are not two issues here, but one. Nor do I see how to go about resolving the latter indecision in a way that differs from my attempt to resolve the former. Appeal to the facts thus turns out to be question begging as a general method for ascertaining truth. For it requires, in effect, that the truth be determined as a condition of its own ascertainment.

The conclusion to which we thus appear driven is that the whole idea of checking beliefs against experience is misguided.

6 On the parallelism of language and reality, see Ludwig Wittgenstein, *Tractatus Logico-Philosophicus* (London: Routledge & Kegan Paul, 1922). For further discussion, see John Passmore, *A Hundred Years of Philosophy* (London: Duckworth, 1957); and Nelson Goodman, "The Way the World Is," *Review of Metaphysics*, 14 (1960), 48–56.

We do not go outside the realm of statements at all. Such is Neu-rath's conclusion, as we have already seen – a conclusion that, however well motivated, must surely be judged unacceptable as an account of science.

3 SCHLICK'S ABSOLUTE FIXED POINTS OF SCIENCE

Convinced of the unacceptability of Neurath's account, Schlick insists that there must be an "unshakeable point of contact be-tween knowledge and reality" (p. 226). To give up "the good old expression 'agreement with reality'" (p. 215) and to espouse in-stead a coherence theory such as that propounded by Neurath yields intolerable consequences:

> If one is to take coherence seriously as a general criterion of truth, then one must consider arbitrary fairy stories to be as true as a historical report, or as statements in a textbook of chemistry, provided the story is constructed in such a way that no contradiction ever arises. (pp. 215–16)

Since the coherence theory allows us to eliminate internal conflict in various ways, yielding "any number of consistent systems of statements which are incompatible with one another" (p. 216), Schlick concludes that "the only way to avoid this absurdity is not to allow any statements whatever to be abandoned or altered, but rather to specify those that are to be maintained, to which the remainder have to be accommodated" (p. 216).

One might suppose, on the basis of such a conclusion, that Schlick would proceed to a defense of the certainty of protocol statements. Not so, however. He grants that such statements, as exemplified by familiar recorded accounts of scientific observa-tion, are indeed subject to error and revision. Even our own pre-viously enunciated protocol statements may be withdrawn. "We grant," writes Schlick,

> that our mind at the moment the judgment was made may have been wholly confused, and that an experience which we now say we had two minutes ago may upon later examination be

found to have been an hallucination, or even one that never took place at all. (p. 213)

Schlick thus agrees with Neurath in denying a privileged role to protocol statements. Like Neurath, he insists that they "have in principle exactly the same character as all the other statements of science: they are hypotheses, nothing but hypotheses" (p. 212). Where, then, is the fixed point of contact between knowledge and reality? Schlick's view is that it is to be located in a special class of statements that are not themselves within science, but are nevertheless essential to its function and, in particular, to its confirmation. His special term for these statements is *Konstatierungen*, though he sometimes calls them "observation statements"; I shall here refer to them uniformly as "confirmation statements."[7]

A confirmation statement is a momentary description of what is simultaneously perceived or experienced. It provides an *occasion* for the production of a protocol statement proper, which is preserved in writing or in memory; it must, however, be sharply distinguished from the protocol statement to which it may give rise. For this protocol statement can no longer describe what is simultaneous with itself; the critical experience has lapsed during the time taken to fix it in writing or memory. The protocol statement, moreover, unlike the confirmation statement, does not die as soon as it is born; its own life extends far beyond the initial point nearest the experience in question. Though it has, to be sure, the advantage of providing an enduring account, the protocol statement is, thus, never more than a hypothesis, subject to interpretation and revision. "For, when we have such a statement before us, it is a mere assumption that it is true, that it agrees with the observation statements [i.e., the confirmation statements] that give rise to it" (pp. 220–1).

Confirmation statements may serve to stimulate the development of genuine scientific hypotheses, but they are too elusive to

---

7 There are problems in choosing a suitable translation; see David Rynin's note on these problems in Ayer, ed., *Logical Positivism*, p. 221. I choose "confirmation statements" to emphasize that statements are thus denoted, in preference to Rynin's "confirmations," though I believe the latter choice follows Schlick's own usage more closely.

be construed as the ultimate and certain *basis* of knowledge. Their contribution consists rather in providing an absolute and indubitable culmination to the process of testing hypotheses. When a predicted experience occurs, and we simultaneously pronounce it to have occurred, we derive "thereby a feeling of *fulfillment*, a quite characteristic satisfaction: we are *satisfied*" (p. 222). Confirmation statements perform their characteristic function when we obtain such satisfaction.

> And it is obtained in the very moment in which the confirmation takes place, in which the observation statement [i.e., confirmation statement] is made. This is of the utmost importance. For thus the function of the statements about the immediately experienced itself lies in the immediate present. Indeed we saw that they have so to speak no duration, that the moment they are gone one has at one's disposal in their place inscriptions, or memory traces, that can play only the role of hypotheses and thereby lack ultimate certainty. One cannot build any logically tenable structure upon the confirmations, for they are gone the moment one begins to construct. If they stand at the beginning of the process of cognition they are logically of no use. Quite otherwise however if they stand at the end; they bring verification (or also falsification) to completion, and in the moment of their occurrence they have already fulfilled their duty. Logically nothing more depends on them, no conclusions are drawn from them. They constitute an absolute end. (p. 222)

In bringing a cycle of testing to an absolute close, a confirmation statement helps to steer the further course of scientific investigation: A falsified hypothesis is rejected and the search for an adequate replacement ensues; a verified hypothesis is upheld and "the formulation of more general hypotheses is sought, the guessing and search for universal laws goes on" (p. 222). The cognitive culmination represented by confirmation statements had, originally, according to Schlick, a purely practical import: It indicated the reliability of underlying hypotheses as to the nature of man's environment, and thus aided man's adjustment to this environment. In science, the joy of confirmation is no longer tied to the "purposes of life" (p. 222), but is pursued for its own sake:

And it is this that the observation statements [confirmation statements] bring about. In them science as it were achieves its goal: it is for their sake that it exists. . . . That a new task begins with the pleasure in which they culminate, and with the hypotheses that they leave behind does not concern them. Science does not rest upon them but leads to them, and they indicate that it has led correctly. They are really the absolute fixed points; it gives us joy to reach them, even if we cannot stand upon them. (p. 223)

What is it, however, that enables confirmation statements to constitute "absolute fixed points"? Schlick conceives these statements as always containing demonstrative terms. His examples are, "Here yellow borders on blue," "Here two black points coincide," "Here now pain." The constituent demonstratives function as gestures. "In order therefore to understand the meaning of such an observation statement [confirmation statement] one must simultaneously execute the gesture, one must somehow point to reality" (p. 225). Thus, he argues, one can understand a confirmation statement "only by, and when, comparing it with the facts, thus carrying out that process which is necessary for the verification of all synthetic statements" (p. 225). For to comprehend its meaning is simultaneously to apprehend the reality indicated by its demonstrative terms:

While in the case of all other synthetic statements determining the meaning is separate from, distinguishable from, determining the truth, in the case of observation statements [confirmation statements] they coincide . . . the occasion of understanding them is at the same time that of verifying them: I grasp their meaning at the same time as I grasp their truth. (p. 225)

The distinctiveness of confirmation statements lies, then, in their immediacy, that is, their capacity to point to a simultaneous experience, in the manner of a gesture. To such immediacy they "owe their value and disvalue; the value of absolute validity, and the disvalue of uselessness as an abiding foundation" (p. 225). It is of the first importance, for Schlick's view, to recognize the distinctiveness of confirmation statements and, in particular, to separate them from protocol statements, for this separation is the key to the problem as he sees it. "Here now blue" is thus not to be confused with the protocol statement of Neurath's type: "M.S. perceived blue on the *nth* of April 1934 at such and such a time and such and such a place." The latter is an uncertain hypothesis, but it is distinct from the former: It must mention a perception and identify an observer. On the other hand, one cannot write down a confirmation statement without altering the meaning of its demonstratives, nor can one formulate an equivalent without demonstratives, for one then "unavoidably substitutes . . . a protocol statement which as such has a wholly different nature" (p. 226).

In sum, if we consider simply the body of scientific statements, they are all hypotheses, all uncertain. To take into account also the relation of this body of statements to reality requires, however, that we acknowledge the special role of confirmation statements as well. An understanding of these statements enables us to see science as "that which it really is, namely, a means of finding one's way among the facts; of arriving at the joy of confirmation, the feeling of finality" (p. 226). These statements do not "lie at the base of science; but like a flame, cognition, as it were, licks out to them, reaching each but for a moment and then at once consuming it. And newly fed and strengthened, it flames onward to the next" (p. 227).

I have already expressed agreement with the critical side of Schlick's doctrine, namely, his rejection of a coherence theory such as Neurath's. But Schlick's positive theory suffers from a variety of fundamental difficulties that render it altogether unacceptable. Consider, first of all, that the coherence view purports to be a theory of science – of "science as a system of statements," as Neurath puts it. Any attempt to restrict the arbitrariness of coherence along the lines of Schlick's diagnosis must specify fixed points to which the statements of science are to be adjusted. It must, that is, specify a fixity to which *science* is responsive, by which *scientific* spontaneity is contained; it must place definite limits upon statement revision within science.

It is just here that Schlick's doctrine fails. For he identifies as "absolute fixed points" only confirmation statements, which fall outside science, and he insists, moreover, that these statements provide no barrier whatever to the revision of scientific statements proper. In particular, Schlick stresses that protocol statements, which are the closest counterparts of confirmation statements within science, "have in principle exactly the same character as all the other statements of science: they are hypotheses, nothing but hypotheses" (pp. 212–13). We have here, it seems, a clear admission that within the realm of science, coherence continues to rule, despite the certainty attributed to confirmation statements. The latter have in effect been so sharply sundered from the body of science that they can yield it no advantage derived from their own presumed fixity.

Nor is it easy to make Schlick's general account of the scientific role of such statements intelligible. They are described as having an essential role in scientific functioning – in particular in the testing and verification of hypotheses. "They bring verification (or also falsification) to completion. . . . Logically nothing more depends on them, no conclusions are drawn from them. They constitute an absolute end" (p. 222). In marking the fulfillment of scientific predictions, confirmation statements are, however, said not only to yield a characteristic satisfaction, but to influence the course of subsequent inquiry: "The hypotheses whose verification ends in them are considered to be upheld, and the formulation of more general hypotheses is sought, the guessing and search for universal laws goes on" (p. 222). The problem is whether these various features ascribed to confirmation statements can be reconciled with one another.

For, on the one hand, these statements constitute an absolute end, having no logical function when standing at the beginning of further cognitive processes, since "the moment they are gone one has at one's disposal in their place inscriptions, or memory traces, that can play only the role of hypotheses and thereby lack ultimate certainty" (p. 222). On the other hand, they enable us to uphold the hypotheses they serve to verify and to reject those they falsify, in either case leading us to conduct subsequent inquiry in a significantly different manner. If, however, a confirmation statement truly constitutes an absolute end, how can it serve thus to qualify our further treatment of relevant hypotheses?

Confirmation statements, it seems, cannot bring testing processes to absolute completion without qualifying further inquiry in a manner precluded by their momentary duration. However, unless they do bring such processes to absolute completion, they have, on Schlick's account, no function at all in the economy of science.

The notion that confirmation statements can have no logical function for subsequent cognitive processes rests on their radical immediacy. To write down a confirmation statement or even to preserve it in memory is, strictly speaking, impossible, for the meaning of critical demonstratives is altered by preservation; moreover, replacement of these demonstratives "by an indication of time and place" inevitably results in the creation of "a protocol statement which as such has a wholly different nature" (p. 226). But immediacy, one may feel, should cut both ways: If it eliminates logical bearing on subsequent processes, it must equally eliminate such bearing on earlier ones. Yet Schlick holds, as we have seen, that confirmation statements bring testing processes to an absolute completion:

> Have our predictions actually come true? In every single case of verification or falsification a "confirmation" [confirmation statement] answers unambiguously with a yes or a no, with joy of fulfillment or disappointment. The confirmations are final. (p. 223)

How can this be? The prediction is, after all, a scientific hypothesis with "a wholly different nature" from that of the confirmation statement in question. How can it derive any benefit from the latter's certainty any more than a later protocol statement can?

Schlick gives, as an example of a prediction, "If at such and such a time you look through a telescope adjusted in such and such a manner you will see a point of light (a star) in coincidence with a black mark (cross wires)" (p. 221). Suppose we now have the confirmation statement "Here now a point of light in coincidence with a black mark." For the sake of argument, let us grant that the latter statement is, at the critical moment, certain. Does it follow that it constitutes an unambiguous and final answer to the question of whether the prediction has in fact come true? Not at all. For the prediction stipulates, in its antecedent clause, certain conditions relating to physical apparatus, time, and the activity of an observer. Unless the experience reported by the confirmation statement is assumed to have occurred in accordance with the conditions thus stipulated, it cannot even be judged relevant to the prediction, much less to fulfill it with finality. On the other hand, if the assumption is made that these conditions have been satisfied in fact, this critical assumption itself shares in the uncertainty of the prediction, being itself clearly no more than a physical hypothesis. The question of whether a prediction has in fact come true is, then, just the question of whether a corrigible scientific statement, rather than a confirmation statement, is true. The alleged certainty of confirmation statements no more enables them to provide absolutely certain completions for earlier scientific processes than it equips them to constitute absolute origins.

The alleged certainty of these statements must, finally, be called into question. According to Schlick, I cannot be deceived regarding the truth of my own confirmation statements, even though, as he writes, "the possibilities of error are innumerable" (p. 212). As he puts it, " 'This here' has meaning only in connection with a gesture" (p. 225). To comprehend the meaning of a confirmation statement, "one must somehow point to reality" (p. 225). It follows, in his view, that I cannot understand a confirmation statement without thereby determining it to be true. Here is the fundamental source of the certainty of confirmation statements: Their understanding presupposes their verification. However, Schlick's conception of the matter rests upon a confusion.

For suppose it be granted that the meaning of demonstrative terms derives from their function as gestures, by which, as Schlick remarks, "the attention is directed upon something observed" (p. 225). Suppose it be admitted that "in order therefore to understand the meaning" of a confirmation statement, "one must simultaneously execute the gesture, one must somehow point to reality" (p. 225). What can be inferred from such admissions? They imply only that the comprehension of a confirmation statement requires attention to those observed elements indicated by its constituent demonstrative terms. In this and this sense only can comprehension of the statement be said to involve a "pointing to reality." By no means is it implied that we must point to reality in the wholly different sense of verifying the attribution represented by the statement as a whole. To equate these senses is to commit a fallacy. Once this fallacy is exposed, Schlick's argument for the certainty of confirmation statements falls to the ground: The understanding of such statements does not, after all, presuppose their verification. I may understand a confirmation statement and be undecided as to its truth; what is more, I can understand, and even affirm, a confirmation statement that is false. Schlick's positive theory, no less than Neurath's, thus proves untenable.

The failure of both these theories may engender despair. For they seem, between them, to exhaust the possibilities for dealing with our basic dilemma between coherence and certainty. Either some of our beliefs must be transparently true of reality and beyond the scope of error and revision, or else we are free to choose any consistent set of beliefs whatever as our own, and to define "correctness" or "truth" accordingly. Either we suppose our beliefs to reflect the facts, in which case we beg the very question of truth and project our language gratuitously upon the world, or else we abandon altogether the intent to describe reality, in which case our scientific efforts reduce to nothing more than a word game.

4 A THIRD WAY

Despite this grim appraisal, I believe that despair is avoidable. My view is that while rejecting certainty, it is yet possible to uphold the referential import of science, that to impose effective constraints upon coherence need beg no relevant questions nor people the world with ghostly duplicates of our language.

Let me turn first to the fundamental opposition between coherence and certainty. We have seen how central this opposition is in the thought of both Neurath and Schlick, who take contrary positions. Schlick and Neurath are, however, agreed in binding extralinguistic reference firmly to certainty, and they join, therefore, in reducing the effective alternatives to two: (1) a rejection of certainty, as well as of appeals to extralinguistic reference, yielding a coherence view, and (2) a rejection of the coherence view in favor of an appeal to extralinguistic reference, yielding a commitment to certainty. But this reduction must itself be rejected. There is, in fact, no need to assume that the alternatives are exhausted by coherence and certainty; a third way lies open.

What is required is simply a steady "referential" limitation upon unbridled coherence; certainty supplies much more than is required. In particular, it imports the notion of a fixity, a freedom from error and consequent revision, which cannot be defended for it is nowhere to be found. We need only recognize that statements have referential values, independent of their consistency relationships to other statements, and that these values, though subject to variation, provide us, *at each moment*, with sufficient "fixity" to constitute a frame of reference for choice of hypotheses.

How are these values of statements, compatible with lack of certainty, to be conceived? They may be thought of as representing our varied inclinations to affirm given statements as true or assert them as scientifically acceptable; equivalently, they may be construed as indicating the initial claims we recognize statements to make upon us, at any given time, for inclusion within our cognitive systems. A notion of this general sort has been put forward by Bertrand Russell in *Human Knowledge,* under the label "intrinsic credibility,"[8] and Nelson Goodman has spoken, analogously, of "initial credibility,"[9] the adjective serving in each case to differentiate the idea in question from the purely relative concept of "probability with respect to certain other statements." Goodman explains his conception as follows:

> Internal coherence is obviously a necessary but not a sufficient condition for the truth of a system. . . . There must be a tie to fact through, it is contended, some immediately certain statements.
>
> Now clearly we cannot suppose that statements derive their credibility from other statements without ever bringing this

8 Bertrand Russell, *Human Knowledge* (New York: Simon & Schuster, 1948), Part 2, Chap. 11, and Part 5, Chaps. 6 and 7.
9 Nelson Goodman, "Sense and Certainty," *Philosophical Review,* 61 (1952), 160–7.

string of statements to earth. . . . So far the argument is
sound. . . . Yet all that is indicated is credibility to some degree,
not certainty. To say that some statements must be initially
credible if any statement is ever to be credible at all is not to say
that any statement is immune to withdrawal. . . . That we have
probable knowledge, then, implies no certainty but only initial
credibility.[10]

The fundamental point for present purposes is this: While certainty is untenable, it is also excessive as a restraint upon
coherence. Such restraint does not require that any of the sentences we affirm be guaranteed to be forever immune to revision;
it is enough that we find ourselves now impelled, in varying
degrees, to affirm and retain them, seeking to satisfy as best we
can the current demands of all. That these current demands vary
for different, though equally consistent statements, and that we
can distinguish, even roughly, the credibility-preserving properties of alternative coherent systems, suffices to introduce a significant limitation upon coherence.

It is the claims of sentences at a given time that set the problem
of systematic adjudication at that time, and so restrain the arbitrariness of coherence. That a sentence may be given up at a
later time does not mean that its present claim upon us may be
blithely disregarded. The idea that once a statement is acknowledged as theoretically revisable, it can carry no cognitive weight
at all is no more plausible than the suggestion that a man loses his
vote as soon as it is seen that the rules make it possible for him to
be outvoted.

The basic dilemma with which we started, between coherence
and certainty, thus collapses. That none of the statements we
assert can be freed of the possibility of withdrawal does not imply
that no statement exercises any referential constraint at any time.
That the statement "There's a horse" cannot be rendered theoretically certain does not permit me to call anything a horse if
only I do not thereby contradict any other statement of mine. On
the contrary, if I have learned the term "horse," I have acquired

10 Ibid., 162–3.

distinctive habits of individuation and classification associated with it; I have learned what Quine refers to as its "built-in mode . . . of dividing [its] reference."[11] These habits do not guarantee that I will never be mistaken in applying the term, but it by no means follows that they do not represent selective constraints upon my mode of employing the term. On the contrary, such constraints generate credibility claims that enter my reckoning critically as I survey my system of beliefs. I seek not consistency alone, but am bound to consider also the relative inclusiveness with which a system honors initial credibilities.

An observational expectation induced in us by our heretofore satisfying system may, for example, be challenged by an experimental observation that drastically increases the credibility of a statement incompatible with this expectation, while radically reducing the credibility of the expectation itself. The problem is to determine which consistent alternative strikes a more inclusive balance of relevant credibility claims. To drop the initial expectation in favor of the more credible incompatible statement demands internal systematic revision in the interests of consistency. To exclude the incompatible statement and maintain the system intact lowers the overall credibility value of the latter, for the credibility loss of its constituent expectation reverberates inward. Every clash–resolution, in short, has its price. In some such situations, the choice may be relatively easy; in others it may be exceedingly delicate; and it may even, in some circumstances, defy resolution.

Nevertheless, it is clear that we are in no case free simply to choose at will among all coherent systems whatever. And, further, it is clear that the control exercised by observation statements does not hinge on certainty. It requires only that the credibility they acquire at particular times be capable of challenging, in the manner previously described, the expectations flowing from other sources. Control is, moreover, released from distinctive ties to any special sort of statement and diffused throughout the realm of statements as a whole.

11 Willard Van Orman Quine, *Word and Object* (New York: Technology Press of MIT and Wiley, 1960), 91.

5 TRUTH AND REALITY

What shall now be said concerning the difficult notions of truth and reality? Eschewing certainty, some philosophers, Neurath included, have rejected all talk of reality and truth. Having pointed out that appeal to an immediate comparison with the facts as a method of ascertaining truth is question begging, and that facts, construed literally as entities, are mere ghostly doubles of true sentences, they have proceeded to cast doubt upon all thought of external reference, as embodied in philosophically innocent talk of reality and fact, and in innocent as well as serious talk of truth. Such skepticism leads, however, to insuperable difficulties, for without external reference, science has no point. If we stay within the circle of statements altogether, we are trapped in a game of words, with which even Neurath (as indicated by his reference to science as an instrument for life) cannot be wholly satisfied. Taken in its extreme form, Neurath's doctrine understandably evokes the sort of criticism that Russell offers:

> Neurath's doctrine, if taken seriously, deprives empirical propositions of all meaning. When I say "the sun is shining," I do not mean that this is one of a number of sentences among which there is no contradiction; I mean something which is not verbal, and for the sake of which such words as "sun" and "shining" were invented. The purpose of words, though philosophers seem to forget this simple fact, is to deal with matters other than words.[12]

One source of the trouble is a persistent confusion between truth and estimation of the truth, between the import of our statements and the processes by which we choose among them. If, for example, appeal to reality or direct comparison with the facts is defective as a method of *ascertaining* truth, this does not show that the *purport* of a true statement cannot properly be described, in

12 Bertrand Russell, *An Inquiry into Meaning and Truth* (London: Allen & Unwin, 1940), pp. 148–9; Penguin ed. (Harmondsworth: Penguin Books, 1962), pp. 140–1.

ordinary language, as "to describe reality" or "to state the facts."
We may have no certain intuition of the truth, but this does not
mean that our statements do not purport to be true. If the sentence "Snow is white" is true, then snow is (really, or in fact)
white, and vice versa, as Tarski insists.[13] As Quine has remarked,
"Attribution of truth in particular to 'Snow is white', for example,
is every bit as clear to us as attribution of whiteness to snow."[14]
We may be unclear as to how to decide whether the sentence
"Snow is white" is true, but the sentence in any case *refers* to snow
and claims it to be white, and if we decide to hold the sentence
to be true, we must be ready to hold snow to be (really, or in
fact) white. Whatever method we employ estimating the truth,
our statements will refer to things quite generally and will purport to attribute to them what, *in reality, or in fact*, is attributable to
them.

There is thus no way of staying wholly within the circle of
statements, for in the very process of deciding which of these to
affirm as true, we are deciding how to refer to, and describe
things, quite generally. The *import of* our statements is inexorably
referential. It is, however, quite another matter to suppose that,
because this is so, the *methodology* by which we accept statements
may be described in terms of an appeal to such supposed entities
as facts, with which candidate statements are to be directly compared. For facts, postulated as special entities corresponding to
truths, are generally suspect, and the determination of their existence is question begging if proposed literally as a method of
ascertaining the truth.

We thus separate the question of the *import* of scientific systems
from the question of the *methods* by which we choose such systems. Can such methods be described without dependence upon
the notion of direct comparison with the facts? Both Neurath and

13 Alfred Tarski, "The Semantic Conception of Truth," *Philosophy and Phenomeno-
logical Research* (1944); reprinted in Herbert Feigl and Wilfrid Sellars, eds.,
Reading in Philosophical Analysis (New York: Appleton-Century-Crofts, 1949),
pp. 52–84.
14 Willard Van Orman Quine, *From a Logical Point of View* (Cambridge, Mass.:
Harvard University Press, 1953), p. 138.

Schlick assume that any conception of science as referential must display such dependence. This supposition, however, is simply false. The conception of credibility above sketched represents a notion of choice among systems of statements, yet makes no use of any idea such as that of comparison with the facts. It is, nevertheless, perfectly compatible with the recognition that any system selected is referential in its *import*. Moreover, credibility considerations rest on the referential values that statements have for us at a given time, that is, on the inclinations we have, at that time, to affirm these statements as true.

Such inclinations as to statements are, surely, tempered by habits of individuation and classification acquired through the social process of learning our particular vocabulary of terms. In learning the term "horse," for example, I have incorporated selective habits of applying and withholding the term; these habits, operating upon what is before me, incline me to a greater or lesser degree to affirm the statement "There's a horse." If I have learned the term "white" as well as "horse," I may, further, be strongly inclined, on a given occasion, to affirm "That horse is white," and my inclination, on such an occasion, will be understandable, in part, as a product of my applying both "horse" and "white" to what I see. I need, however, surely not recognize any such additional entity as *the fact that that horse is white,* nor need I have an applicable term for such a supposed entity in my vocabulary. Though it hinges in various ways on referential habits associated with a given vocabulary, the notion of initial credibility thus requires no reference to *facts,* in particular.

To be sure, whether I am to accept a statement depends not only on my initial inclination to accept it, but also on its fitting coherently within a system of beliefs that is sufficiently preserving of relevant credibilities. Here again, however, there is no reference to any such entities as facts, with which statements are to be compared. In accepting a system, I nevertheless take its *import* to be referential: I hold its statements to be true and genuinely accept whatever attributions it makes to the entities mentioned in these statements. In a philosophically harmless sense, I may then say that I take the system as expressive of the facts. I have, at no time, any guarantees that my system will stand the test of the future, but the continual task of present evaluation is the only task it is possible for me to undertake. Science, generally, prospers not through seeking impossible guarantees, but through striving to systematize credibly a continuously expanding experience.

Chapter 13
Worlds and versions

Goodman's *Ways of Worldmaking* initiated a new chapter in the consideration of relations between the world and its representations, or – as he prefers to call them – versions. In his book he defends the view that there actually are many worlds if any, and that we make these worlds by making versions, using previous versions as our resources. In what follows, I offer an account of Goodman's treatment and criticize his view of worldmaking in its objectual interpretation.

1 THE WONDERFUL WORLDS OF GOODMAN

"Worldmaking," Goodman tells us, "begins with one version and ends with another."[1] Is worldmaking, then, simply the making of versions – that is, descriptions, depictions, or other representations – and are worlds to be construed just as versions? The answer does not lie on the surface. The term "world" is nowhere defined in the book and an examination of the passages in which the term appears yields two conflicting interpretations: On the first, or *versional*, interpretation, a world is a true (or right) world-

---

"Worlds and Versions" appeared as "The Wonderful Worlds of Goodman," *Synthese*, 45 (1980), 201–9.
1 Nelson Goodman, *Ways of Worldmaking* (Indianapolis, Ind.: Hackett, 1978), p. 97. From here on, all page references to this book will be given in parentheses following their respective citations in the text.

version, and the pluralism defended simply reflects, and extends to versions generally, the *Structure of Appearance* doctrine that conflicting systematizations can be found for any prephilosophical subject matter. On the second, or *objectual,* interpretation, a world is a realm of things (versions or nonversions) referred to or described by (p. 119) a right world-version. Pluralistic talk of worlds is here not simply talk of conflicting versions; "multiple actual worlds" is Goodman's watchword and he cautions us that it should not "be passed over as purely rhetorical" (p. 110).[2]

2 WORLDS AS VERSIONS

Each of these two interpretations of "worlds" can call upon implicit as well as explicit statements in support. Take first the versional interpretation. After suggesting that sometimes a cluster of versions rather than a single version may constitute a world (itself a nonobjectual view), Goodman says, "But for many purposes, right world-descriptions and world-depictions and world-perceptions, the ways-the-world-is, or just versions, can be treated as our worlds" (p. 4). "In what non-trivial sense," he goes on to ask, "are there . . . many worlds?" And he answers, "Just this, I think: that many different world-versions are of independent interest and importance, without any requirement or presumption of reducibility to a single base" (p. 4). Worlds are here right world-versions, and the multiplicity of worlds is the multiplicity of such world-versions. Clinching this interpretation, Goodman then introduces his treatment of "ways of worldmaking" as follows: "With false hope of a firm foundation gone, *with the world displaced by worlds that are but versions* . . . we face the questions how *worlds* are made, tested, and known" (p. 7, my italics). The basic discussion that follows of "processes that go into worldmaking" (p. 7) is, then, to be understood as concerned with versions rather than with things, objects, or realms described

2 For the *versional* but not the *objectual* interpretation, "world" is always, strictly speaking, short for "world-version," a compound in which the constituent "world" is syncategorematic and nonreferential, its position inaccessible to variables of quantification.

by them, and the testing and making of worlds is to be construed as the testing and making of versions.

That it is versions that are at stake is implicit throughout this discussion, where the individuation of worlds is said at times to hinge on the concepts and distinctions available to relevant groups of persons (p. 9), on emphasis and accent (p. 11), on relevant kinds (p. 11), on ordering (p. 12), and on modes of organization *"built into a world"* (p. 14). "Worlds not differing in entities . . . may differ in ordering" (p. 12), says Goodman, thus distinguishing worlds where there is no difference whatever in the things denoted. He allows indeed that "a green emerald and a grue one, *even if the same emerald* . . . belong to worlds organized into different kinds" (p. 11, my italics, see also p. 101). Now since Goodman explicitly upholds the nominalistic principle "no difference without a difference of individuals" (p. 95), when he here differentiates worlds simply by the order or emphasis of versions or the kinds indicated by them, he must be referring neither to the realms of individuals described, nor, surely, to various abstract entities associated with them, but rather to the versions themselves.

The point is strikingly illustrated by two contrasting discussions of the question of variant histories – one in Goodman's early paper "A World of Individuals"[3] and the other in *Ways of Worldmaking*. In the first of these discussions, he writes, "We do not take the varied histories of the Battle of Bull Run as recounting different occurrences. In daily life a multiplicity of descriptions is no evidence for a corresponding multiplicity of things described."[4] On the other hand, in *Ways of Worldmaking*, he says of "two histories of the Renaissance: one that, without excluding the battles, stresses the arts; and another that, without excluding the arts, stresses the battles" that "this difference in style is a difference in weighting that gives us *two different Renaissance worlds* (p. 101–2, my italics). Consistency with the nominalist

3 N. Goodman, "A World of Individuals," *The Problem of Universals* (Notre Dame, Ind.: University of Notre Dame Press, 1956), pp. 13–31; reprinted in Goodman, *Problems and Projects* (Indianapolis, Ind.: Bobbs-Merrill, 1972), pp. 155–72.
4 Goodman, *Problems and Projects*, p. 164.

principle demands that the worlds mentioned in this last quotation not be construed as comprising the described occurrences, but that they be taken rather as versional.

3 WORLDS AS OBJECTS

Let us now turn to the objectual interpretation of worlds. Goodman speaks of "the many stuffs – matter, energy, waves, phenomena – that worlds are made of" (p. 6), and the presumption of the passage is that he is not simply referring to the inscriptions constituting versions. He uses the adjective "actual" to modify "worlds," characterizing the "multiple worlds" he countenances as "just the actual worlds . . . *answering to* true or right versions" (p. 94, my italics), the natural reading of "answering to" being "denoted by," "referred to," "compliant with," or "described by." Goodman indeed expressly distinguishes between "versions that do and those that do not refer," and he insists that we want "to talk about the things and *worlds,* if any, *referred* to" (p. 96, my italics). Furthermore, he introduces the notion of truth "in a given actual world," holding that a statement is true in such a world if "true insofar as that world alone is taken into consideration" (p. 110). Here, "world" presumably cannot be intended as world-version, as is further implicit in the following consideration: He remarks that conflicting statements cannot be taken as "true in the same world without admitting all statements whatsoever . . . as true in the same world, and that world itself as impossible" (p. 110). Were "world" to be taken in this passage as "world-version," there would here be no impossibility whatever – only inconsistency.

Goodman explains both truth and rightness in terms of *fitting a world:* "A statement is true, and a description or representation right, for a world it fits" (p. 132), he declares. Like the notion of "answering to," that of "fit" appears also to be a semantic idea, and the related use of "world" clearly objectual rather than versional.

The objectual interpretation is necessitated, finally, by those passages in which Goodman explicitly treats worlds as comprised of *ranges of application* of predicates, or as consisting of the *realms* of different versions. In this vein, he writes:

> The statements that the Parthenon is intact and that it is ruined are both true – for different temporal parts of the building; and the statement that the apple is white and that it is red are both true – for different spatial parts of the apple. . . . In each of these cases, the two *ranges of application* combine readily into a recognized kind or object; and the two statements are true in different parts or subclasses of the same *world*. (p. 111, my italics)

Clearly, the reference here is not to different parts or subclasses of the same version.

This example concerned ranges of application; consider now the reference to worlds as *realms*. Discussing two geometrical systems with rival accounts of points, Goodman asserts that if they are both true, they are so in different realms – the first "in our sample space taken as consisting solely of lines" and the second "in that space taken as consisting solely of points." For more comprehensive versions that conflict similarly, he says that "their *realms* are thus less aptly regarded as within one world than as *two different worlds*" (p. 116, my italics). The reference of "worlds" in this passage is not to versions but to things to which versions apply; the interpretation here, in short, is objectual.

4 ARE WORLDS MADE?

Now the versional and the objectual interpretations of worlds do not mix; they are in conflict. As we have seen, the idea of different Renaissance worlds emerging from variant histories cannot be objectual, since their realms of application are assumed identical. Conversely, the versional interpretation is precluded by the notion of actual worlds *referred to* by true versions, since such versions in fact refer to all sorts of things, nonversions as well as versions.

Goodman seems to hold, indeed, that these conflicting interpretations of "worlds" reflect the vacillations of antecedent theoretical practice. The line drawn by such practice between "versionizing" and "objectifying" is, he believes, not a hard but a variable line, motivated by convenience and convention. "In practice," he writes, "we draw the line wherever we like, and change it as often as suits our purposes. On the level of theory, we flit back and forth between extremes as blithely as a physicist between particle and field theories. When the verbiage view threatens to dissolve everything into nothing, we insist that all true versions describe worlds. When the right-to-life sentiment threatens an overpopulation of worlds, we call it all talk" (p. 119). Yet the availability of these two interpretations – however the line may be drawn – makes it important to examine closely Goodman's thesis that worlds are made. I can accept this thesis with "worlds" taken versionally, but I find it impossible to accept otherwise.

5 WORLDMAKING: VERSIONAL YES, OBJECTUAL NO

That Goodman himself intends worldmaking to be taken both ways is shown in a variety of passages. In a summary statement toward the end of the book, he says:

> Briefly, then truth of statements and rightness of descriptions, representations, exemplifications . . . is primarily a matter of fit: fit to what is *referred* to in one way or another, or to *other renderings*, or to modes and manners of organization. The differences between *fitting a version to a world, a world to a version, and a version together or to other versions* fade when the role of versions in *making the worlds they fit* is recognized. (p. 138, my italics)

Moreover, Goodman specifically speaks of worlds, taken objectually, as made. In a crucial passage, he writes, "We make worlds by making versions. . . . The multiple worlds I countenance are just the actual worlds made by and answering to true or right versions" (p. 94). That this passage requires the objectual interpretation is shown by the mention of worlds as *answering* to true versions. Thus, in saying we make worlds by making versions, Goodman is not uttering the triviality that we make versions by making them. Can he then be asserting rather that in making right versions we make what they refer to – that is, in making true descriptions we make what they describe, in making applicable words we make what they denote?

Apparently, the answer is yes. "Of course," he writes,

> we want to distinguish between versions that do and those that do not refer, and to talk about the things and worlds, if any, referred to: but these things and worlds and even the stuff they are made of – matter, anti-matter, mind, energy, or what not – are fashioned along with the versions themselves. (p. 96)

Here he clearly says that we make not only versions but also the things they refer to and even the material of which these things are made.

Now the claim that it is we who made the stars by making the word "star" I consider absurd, taking this claim in its plain and literal sense. It mistakes a feature of discourse for a feature of the subject of discourse – a mistake Goodman himself has warned against in an earlier paper,[5] and it seems to conflict with his own insistence on the difference between a version and what it refers to. Goodman himself emphasizes (p. 94) that his "willingness to accept countless alternative true or right world-versions does not mean that everything goes . . . that truths are no longer distinguished from falsehoods." Since, as I believe, the claim that we made the stars is false if anything is, his version of versions is itself false if it implies this claim. Nor is it helpful to say that we made the stars *as* stars – that before the word "star" existed, stars did not exist qua stars. For, in the first place, that stars did not exist qua stars does not imply that they did not exist, or that we made them. And in the second place, the existence of stars qua stars is just their existence plus their being called "stars." No one disputes that before we had the word "stars," stars weren't called

---

5 "Philosophers sometimes mistake features of discourse for features of the subject of discourse. We seldom conclude that the world consists of words just because a true description of it does, but we sometimes suppose that the structure of the world is the same as the structure of the description." Ibid., p. 24.

"stars," but that doesn't mean they didn't exist. It would be altogether misleading on this basis alone to say we *made* them.[6]

But a deeper philosophical motivation underlies Goodman's notion of worldmaking. A pervasive theme in his work is the rejection of both the given and the notion of a "ready-made world that lies waiting to be described" (p. 132). He urges again and again that the organization of our concepts and categories is not unique, that such "modes of organization . . . are not 'found in the world' but *built into a world*" (pp. 12–14, esp. 14). The supposition is perhaps that unless we take our star-versions to have made the stars, we will be driven to accept either a neutral given without concepts altogether or else the preexistence of our conceptual scheme to the exclusion of all others. While agreeing with the underlying philosophical motivation, I cannot, however, see that the latter supposition is sound. That stars existed before people implies nothing about concepts, their uniqueness or preexistence. Star-concepts did not, but stars did, antedate the emergence of living creatures. Star-concepts were surely not ready-made, waiting to be used; they were indeed made by us. It doesn't follow that the stars were therefore made by us rather than in fact (but in a metaphorical sense) waiting to be described. To reject the given and to allow a multiplicity of conceptual schemes does not require objectual worldmaking.

The objectual version of worldmaking may, however, perhaps have another philosophical source in Goodman's view of *facts* – more particularly his recognition of how vocabulary constrains and shapes our factual descriptions. The topic arises in his discussion of the phenomenon of apparent motion, that is, the seeing of a moving light where there are, physically, just two distinct flashes, the one following the other a short distance away.

6 Goodman, *Languages of Art* (Indianapolis, Ind.: Hackett, 1968, 1976), p. 88, defends himself against the charge that he makes what a picture expresses depend upon what is said about it, thus "crediting the expression achieved not to the artist but to the commentator." He writes: " 'Sad' may apply to a picture even though no one ever happens to use the term in describing the picture; and calling a picture sad by no means *makes* it so" (my italics). Exactly. "Star" may apply to something even though no one ever happens to use the term in describing it; and calling something a star by no means makes it one.

Discussing the case of certain subjects who report not seeing the apparent motion, Goodman asks whether they are not perhaps indeed aware of it, but taking it as a *sign* of the physical sequence of light flashes – that is, *looking through* the phenomenal to the physical state, "as we take the oval appearance of the table top as a sign that it is round" (p. 92). Can this possibility be tested? Can such subjects be brought to report directly on their actual perceptual experience? To ask them "to avoid all conceptualization" would be useless, since it would leave them "speechless." Rather, as Goodman suggests, "The best we can do is to specify the sort of terms, the vocabulary" to be used, instructing the subjects to describe what they see "in perceptual or phenomenal rather than physical terms." And this, says Goodman, "casts an entirely different light on what is happening. That the instruments to be used in fashioning the facts must be specified makes pointless any identification of the physical with the real and of the perceptual with the merely apparent" (p. 92). He concludes, further, that we must not say "both are versions of the same facts" in any sense that implies that "there are independent facts of which both are versions" (p. 93).

There are then, for Goodman, no independent facts, construed as entities discrete from versions and their objects. What then does his talk of "fashioning the facts" (p. 92) come to? Presumably this: that the true reports of observations giving descriptions of such objects are constrained by the vocabularies employed; these vocabularies are thus instruments for creating factual descriptions. Since all our knowledge of objects is, moreover, embodied in such descriptions, our knowledge is, itself, in the same way, shaped by our vocabularies. But what are objects themselves? We have no access to objects aside from our knowledge of them; they are therefore themselves shaped by our vocabularies. For this reason, we can say that, in making our versions, we make their objects. Possibly some such line of reasoning motivates Goodman's objectual worldmaking.

Whether it does or not, I do not myself find it convincing. Even were it true that we have no access to objects aside from our knowledge of them, it would not follow that objects are made by our knowledge. Moreover, to say we have no access to, or contact with, objects aside from our knowledge of them is true only if by "access" we intend such things as understanding and awareness, that is, "cognitive access." Thus, the statement is trivial; it assures us that we can have knowledge of objects only in having knowledge of them. And to say that our knowledge of objects is shaped by our vocabularies boils down to saying that the descriptions we compose are made up of the words we have. From this triviality it clearly does not follow that we create or shape the things to which our words refer, or determine that our descriptions shall be true. In making the true statement that there were stars before men, we do not also make the stars that were there then.

Now, Goodman himself insists on the separation of truth from falsehood; as we have seen, he denies "that everything goes" (p. 94). There are, he asserts, false as well as true versions; he rules out the idea that any version can be made true at will. And his discussion of fiction indeed offers concrete examples of such constraints. "Some depictions and descriptions," he writes, "do not literally denote anything. Painted or written portrayals of Don Quixote, for example, do not denote Don Quixote – who is *simply not there* to be denoted" (p. 103, my italics). The creation of a Don Quixote–version evidently does not automatically create an object for it. The mere making of the word does not guarantee it will be non-null. Whether there is or is not an object satisfying a version of our making is thus not, in general, up to us. Whether a world answers to a version is, in general, independent of what we may wish or will. How then can Goodman describe his "actual worlds" as both "made by" and "answering to true or right versions"? How can he say "we make worlds by making versions" (p. 94)? I conclude that he cannot and that, despite his disclaimer (p. 110), objectual talk of worldmaking had *better* be taken as "purely rhetorical."

Chapter 14

World-features and discourse-dependence

I offer now some further comments on my controversy with Nelson Goodman regarding worldmaking.[1] Let me begin with a preliminary remark: I don't much like the elastic term "world" and do not want to be taken as defending some doctrine about the world – arguing that there really is one world, or that the world is the touchstone of truth, or independent of mind, or the like. I should not wish to express any of my philosophical convictions by using this term in a primitive, literal, and essential way. My references employing the term are wholly addressed, in critical vein, to Goodman's uses, or else are to be cashed out by terms denoting more limited and more comprehensible entities. For this reason, I introduced reference to stars, about which sensible and scientifically sound things can be said – for example, that in any case stars were not made by men.

Another preliminary point is this: I do not dispute the sort of relativism, or pluralism, propounded in Goodman's *Structure of Appearance*,[2] for which, given any prephilosophical subject matter, there are likely to be conflicting though adequate systematizations, the points of conflict falling in the region of "don't cares."

"World-Features and Discourse-Dependence" is drawn from my *Inquiries* (Indianapolis, Ind.: Hackett, 1986), pp. 82–5.

1 See Chapter 13, this volume, and Goodman's response to the original paper given in *Synthese*, 45 (1980), 211–15, and again in his book *Of Mind and Other Matters* (Cambridge, Mass.: Harvard University Press, 1984), pp. 40–2.
2 Nelson Goodman, *The Structure of Appearance*, 3d ed. (Dordrecht: Reidel, 1977).

The existence of such systematizations underlies Goodman's espousal of extensional isomorphism rather than identity as a criterion of adequacy for what he calls "constructional systems." Thus, a systematic definition of points as certain classes of lines does not establish that points are identical with such classes, but only that relative to our purpose to preserve certain prephilosophical "cares," they do not need to be construed as nonidentical with them. We can, indeed, compatibly say something similar concerning a conflicting systematic definition of points as certain classes of volumes. There is, in this sort of account in *The Structure of Appearance*, no talk of worlds at all and certainly no talk of worldmaking, although the same form of relativism shines through.

What I criticize in my paper is not such relativism, but the later, accreted talk of worlds and their making, construed "objectually" and not simply "versionally." I find no difficulty in taking worlds to be made, *if* by "worlds" one means versions. But I cannot see how one can suppose worlds to be made, if by "worlds" one means things "answering to true versions" – including, as Goodman says, "matter, anti-matter, mind, energy, or what not . . . fashioned along with the versions themselves."[3] Now Goodman does not define "world" in his book, and he uses it ambiguously, drawing what I can only consider cold comfort from the alleged fact that physicists' talk is also ambiguous. But when he insists that worlds are literally made, in *both* of the interpretations he gives to this claim, I conclude that he can avoid outright falsity only by such an unnatural construal of "made" as to cause high philosophical mischief. My paper offers a variety of considerations in support of my argument, to which Goodman offers five main replies.[4]

First, he admits to the ambiguity in his use of the term "world," arguing that, though conflicting, the versional and objectual interpretations are equally right and often interchangeable. But I do

---

3 Nelson Goodman, *Ways of Worldmaking* (Indianapolis, Ind.: Hackett, 1978).
4 Goodman's replies are from his *Of Mind and Other Matters*, to which page numbers in text refer.

not object to mere ambiguity, which can as a rule be cleared up with sufficient care and the refinement of terminology.

Second, he says:

> We cannot find any world-feature independent of all versions. Whatever can be said truly of a world is dependent on the saying – not that whatever we say is true but that whatever we say truly . . . is nevertheless informed by and relative to the language or other symbol system we use. No firm line can be drawn between world-features that are discourse-dependent and those that are not. (p. 41)

The trouble with this reply is that it appeals to the notion of a feature. But what *is* a feature? I presume that for a nominalist such as Goodman, features will not be properties or classes but terms or predicates, construed as, or constituted by, tokens of one or another sort. Then, of course, features will obviously be dependent on the saying – that is, brought forth by the process of token production. Indeed, whatever we say, whether truly *or* falsely, will in this sense be dependent on the saying, informed by and relative to our language or symbolism. However, whether a feature or predicate of our making is *null or not* is not in the same way dependent on the saying; whether a statement is true or not is, as Goodman agrees, independent of our saying. Thus if by a *world*-feature, Goodman means a feature that is not null in fact, then that any given feature *is* a world-feature is indeed independent of our version. Its status *as* a world-feature is *not* discourse dependent.

Third, Goodman suggests that it is fallacious to assume "that whatever we make we can make any way we like" (p. 41). I agree in rejecting this assumption. I certainly do not deny the difficulty of making a true or right version. What I deny is that by making a true version we make that to which it refers.

In *Ways of Worldmaking*, Goodman speaks of "actual worlds made by and answering to true or right versions."[5] Now, whether a world answers to a version of our making is, in general, not up

5 Goodman, *Ways of Worldmaking*, p. 94.

199

to us. Thus, if an "actual world" answers to a version of our making, we can hardly be supposed to have made it do so. Moreover, if a version of our making turns out to be true, it hardly follows that we have made its object. Neither Pasteur nor his version of the germ theory made the bacteria he postulated, nor was Neptune created either by Adams and Leverrier or by their prescient computations.

Fourth, Goodman asks me "which features of the stars we did not make" (p. 42) and challenges me "to state how these differ from features clearly dependent on discourse" (p. 42). Surely we made the words by which we describe stars; that these words are discourse dependent is trivially true. But the fact that the word "star" is non-null is not therefore of our making; its discourse-dependence does not imply our making it happen that there *are* stars or, in short, our making the stars: It doesn't imply that the *stars* are *themselves* discourse dependent. Goodman writes, in *Languages of Art*, " 'Sad' may apply to a picture even though no one ever happens to use the term in describing the picture; and calling a picture sad by no means makes it so."[6] Analogously, "star" may apply to something even though no one ever happens to use the term in describing it; and calling something a star by no means makes it one.

Finally, Goodman tries to dispel the absurdity of supposing that we made the stars by arguing that we made "a space and time that contains those stars. . . . We make a star as we make a constellation, by putting its parts together and marking off its boundaries" (p. 42). I find this singularly unconvincing. We have surely made the scientific schemes by which we formulate temporal and spatial descriptions, but to say that we have therefore made space and time can be no less absurd than to say we made the stars. Nor did we make the Big Dipper or Orion merely by defining their respective boundaries.

Goodman concludes by saying:

We do not make stars as we make bricks; not all making is a matter of molding mud. The worldmaking mainly in question

6 Nelson Goodman, *Languages of Art* (Indianapolis, Ind.: Hackett, 1976), p. 88.

here is making not with hands but with minds, or rather with languages or other symbol systems. Yet when I say that worlds are made, I mean it literally. . . . Surely we make versions, and right versions make worlds. (p. 42)

The suggestion here is that my critique of worldmaking construes it as a physical rather than a symbolic process.

But my argument is altogether independent of this contrast. My claim is that in any normal understanding of the words, we did not make the stars, whether by hand, mind, or symbol. Certainly, we make things with minds; we thus make words, symbols, versions. The issue is whether in thus making star-descriptions we also make stars. To propose, as Goodman does, that we may be said to make something whenever we devise a true description for it is certainly possible, even if wildly unnatural; we can certainly make language mean anything we want it to mean. But such a proposal seems to me unusually mischievous in inviting confusions, paradoxes, and misunderstandings – and encouraging an overblown voluntarism. And it blurs the ordinary distinction between making an omelet and writing a recipe for one. Rather than Goodman's "We make versions, and right versions make worlds," I would rather adopt the slogan "We make versions, and things (made by others, by us, or by no one) make them right."

Chapter 15

Worries about worldmaking

I have learned so much from Nelson Goodman over the years, and I have so much respect for his work, that our disagreement about worldmaking comes as something of a surprise to us both. Yet this disagreement has survived our various exchanges of the past 14 years and so must, I suspect, indicate some deep-seated misunderstanding or conflict of visions. I here respond to his most recent paper on the issue, "On Some Worldly Worries,"[1] and say why worldmaking does indeed cause me to worry.

1 A PRELIMINARY REGRET

Goodman begins by saying he is going to consider arguments raised in my book *Inquiries*,[2] which I had not raised in my earlier paper, "The Wonderful Worlds of Goodman."[3] There are indeed such additional arguments in my book,[4] but I regret to say that Goodman does not address these at all, considering only points

"Worries about Worldmaking" appears in Peter McCormick, ed., *Starmaking* (Boston: M.I.T. Press, 1996).

1 Nelson Goodman, "On Some Worldly Worries," published by the author at Emerson Hall, Harvard University, Cambridge, Mass. September 1, 1988, pp. 1–5. Also *Synthese*, 95 (1993), 9–12.

2 Israel Scheffler, *Inquiries* (Indianapolis, Ind.: Hackett, 1986). See Chapter 14, this volume.

3 Israel Scheffler, "The Wonderful Worlds of Goodman," *Synthese*, 45 (1980), 201–9. See Chapter 13, this volume.

4 On pages 82–5. See Chapter 14, this volume.

found in my earlier paper. Had he addressed these new arguments, might he have found them persuasive?

2 THE QUESTION OF ORDER

In my paper, I offer some ancillary considerations to illustrate Goodman's treatment of "worlds" as sometimes versional, sometimes objectual. Since this variable treatment is explicitly affirmed by Goodman,[5] the disposition of my ancillary illustrations does not bear on the main point, that is, the variable treatment, which is not in contention. Nevertheless, let us consider the two particular illustrations I offered, both related to the individuation of worlds by ordering.

Goodman writes, "Worlds not differing in entities . . . may differ in ordering."[6] On this, I commented that worlds differentiated by their ordering alone must be versions if his nominalistic principle ("no difference without a difference of individuals") is to be upheld. He now replies by distinguishing enduring entities from their time slices, arguing:

> Given five square cards, surely different arrangements of them may yield wholes of different shapes; and if the cards bear certain letter inscriptions, a reordering may turn "cause" into "sauce". But what we speak of here as a difference in arrangement of the (enduring) cards amounts to a difference in arrangement between *different temporal parts* of the cards. . . . Confusion arises from an ellipsis in ordinary speech; what we speak of as a difference in arrangement of cards amounts, more explicitly, to a difference in arrangement between different temporal parts of the cards.[7]

But it is Goodman himself, after all, who spoke of worlds not differing in *entities* yet differing in ordering. Can he himself thus

5 See, e.g., his *Of Minds and Other Matters* (Cambridge, Mass.: Harvard University Press, 1984), p. 41, "We can have it both ways. To say that every right version is a world and to say that every right version has a world answering to it may be equally right even if they are at odds with each other."

6 Goodman, *Ways of Worldmaking* (Indianapolis, Ind.: Hackett, 1978), p. 12.

7 Goodman, "On Some Worldly Worries," p. 1.

now be claiming to have traded on the confusion he mentions, by taking the neutral word "entities" to refer to the enduring individuals whose time slice sums (but not they themselves) may yet differ from one another? Goodman says, "Nothing here violates the nominalistic principle."[8] My intent was not to show a violation but to argue that if worlds not differing in entities yet differ in ordering, they must be construed as versions. And the main point, that is, that Goodman at times takes "worlds" as "world-versions," is not here at issue.

Much the same can be said of my argument that in allowing varied histories to determine different worlds, Goodman was apparently interpreting worlds as versional. This argument was not, as Goodman terms it, a "complaint";[9] it was not intended, as he apparently thinks, to show an inconsistency. The point was rather to illustrate his versional use of "worlds."

He now replies that although "varied histories of the battle of Bull Run are no evidence for a multiplicity of things described," two histories of the Renaissance may indeed "give us two different Renaissance worlds." This is so, he says, because his operative principle is not "different right versions, different worlds" but rather "*disagreeing* right versions, different worlds (if any)."[10]

Does this reply then imply that the two histories of the Renaissance yielding different worlds disagree in the occurrences they denote, so that "worlds" in his usage here is to be understood as objectual after all? This seems to run counter to his description of the variance between the histories, which he terms a "difference in style . . . a difference in weighting," where one history, "*without excluding the battles,* stresses the arts," while the other "*without excluding the arts,* stresses the battles."[11] I conclude from this passage not that he is inconsistent, but that he is here treating "worlds" with versional rather than objectual reference. I am, however, content to leave the last word on this and the previous

8 Ibid.
9 Ibid.
10 Ibid., p. 2.
11 Goodman, *Ways of Worldmaking,* pp. 101–2.

example to Goodman. However he decides them, no disagreement remains over the main point that he sometimes takes "worlds" as "world-versions."

3 WHAT DISTURBS ME

Goodman says I am "disturbed" by his saying "that a term or picture or other version is ordinarily different from what it denotes and yet also that talk of worlds tends to be interchangeable with talk of right versions."[12] I am in fact not at all disturbed by this sort of statement, the flavor of which has become widely familiar through Tarski's semantic criterion of truth. Thus, Goodman writes:

> A version saying that there is a star up there is not itself bright or far off, and the star is not made up of letters. On the other hand, saying that there is a star up there and saying that the statement "There is a star up there" is true amount, trivially, to much the same thing, even though the one seems to talk about a star and the other to talk about a statement.[13]

Rather, what disturbs me is what Goodman has himself criticized, that is, "philosophers [who] sometimes mistake features of discourse for features of the subject of discourse." As he continues, "We seldom conclude that the world consists of words just because a true description of it does."[14] And here I would add that we seldom conclude that the world is made by us just because a true description of it is.

I can understand the making of words but not the making thereby of the worlds they refer to. I can accept that versions are made but not that the "things and worlds and even the stuff they are made of – matter, anti-matter, mind, energy, or what not – are fashioned along with the versions themselves."[15]

12 Goodman, "On Some Worldly Worries," p. 2.
13 Goodman, *Of Mind and Other Matters*, p. 41.
14 Goodman, *Problems and Projects* (Indianapolis, Ind.: Bobbs-Merrill, 1972), p. 24.
15 Goodman, *Ways of Worldmaking*, p. 96.

4 MULTIPLICITY YES, WORLDMAKING NO

Goodman thinks that what "bothers" me is "talk of multiple worlds or conflicting right versions or worldmaking."[16] He is right about the third item but not about the first two. Here I believe he just misunderstands me.

I remarked favorably on the "multiplicity of conceptual schemes" in my original paper[17] and affirmed its consistency with a rejection of objectual worldmaking. I certainly have no quarrel with the sort of relativism propounded in Goodman's *Structure of Appearance*[18] and agree completely with his statement "that many different world-versions are of independent interest and importance, without any requirement or presumption of reducibility to a single base."[19]

I am as opposed to any such requirement or presumption as he is; my argument is not with his pluralism or relativism but with his voluntarism. More particularly, what I criticize is his affirmation of the making of worlds, objectually construed, whether one or many. "We make versions," says Goodman, "and right versions make worlds."[20] But I say: we make versions but we do not make them right.

5 TIME

To the question "how a star that existed before all versions could be made by a version," Goodman responds by appealing to the relativity of time. He imagines a version for which "the star and everything else come into being only *via* a version."[21]

Now, the mere possibility of such a version is radically weaker than Goodman's categorical claim that right versions make worlds. The latter claim already presumes a version that places

16 Goodman, "On Some Worldly Worries," p. 4.
17 See Scheffler, *Inquiries*, p. 276. See also Chapter 13, this volume.
18 See Scheffler, *Inquiries*, pp. 271 and 83. See also Chapters 13 and 14, this volume.
19 Goodman, *Ways of Worldmaking*, p. 4.
20 Goodman, *Of Mind and Other Matters*, p. 42.
21 Goodman, "On Some Worldly Worries," pp. 3–4.

versions before stars and does not merely assert its possibility. But nowhere are the details of such a fantastic version, which would require fundamental alterations in "any of our trusted world-versions," spelled out. Nor is an argument forthcoming to show that the effort to produce a workable version along these lines could in fact be carried through. Finally, Goodman asks whether this hypothetical version or one of our familiar versions is right, and he answers, "Both."[22] He is thus apparently prepared to relinquish his categorical claim altogether.

6 GOODMAN'S DIALOGUE

Goodman hopes to clinch his case for worldmaking by offering "a fragmentary dialogue." The critical conclusion of the dialogue has Goodman's protagonist saying, "But do stars-not-*qua*-stars, stars-not-*qua*-moving and not-*qua*-fixed move or not? Without a version, they are neither moving nor fixed. And whatever neither moves nor is fixed, is neither *qua* so-and-so nor *qua* not so-and-so, comes to nothing."[23]

Of course, whoever writes an imaginary dialogue determines the outcome. I should myself rephrase the concluding passage as follows: But do stars not yet called "stars," stars not yet describable as moving or as fixed, move or not? Without a language capable of describing anything as a star we cannot call a star "a star"; without the language to describe anything as moving or as fixed, we cannot describe a star as moving or as fixed.

Given the language to do so, we may, however, of course decide to describe a star as moving, even as having moved before we acquired our language. But acquiring such language does not automatically ensure its applicability to any given instance. Acquiring the word "moving" does not in itself determine that it is non-null. We certainly do not claim that the later origination of our language caused the star to move then. Nevertheless, we may truly describe it as having moved then.

22 Ibid., p. 4.
23 Ibid., pp. 2–3.

7 COUNTER-DIALOGUE

As an alternative to Goodman's dialogue, I offer the following counter-dialogue, to bring out my main point:

"The Big Dipper was made by our adopted world version."

"You mean, I suppose, that this version contains the applicable term 'Big Dipper'?"

"Yes."

"And does the containing of that term imply that our version actually made the Big Dipper itself?"

"Exactly. As Goodman has said, 'We make worlds by making versions.'"[24]

"Does the containing of the term 'Don Quixote' in an adopted version similarly imply that the version actually made Don Quixote?"

"Of course not. As Goodman has written, 'Painted or written portrayals of Don Quixote . . . do not denote Don Quixote – who is simply not there to be denoted.'"[25]

"Then a version may contain terms that are null as well as terms that are non-null whose objects are either there or not there?"

"I have just said as much. But the Big Dipper version is true, while the Don Quixote version is false."

"By that you mean that the term 'Big Dipper' is non-null while the term 'Don Quixote' is null?"

"I guess so."

"Then the non-null character of 'Big Dipper' (i.e., the truth of its containing version) is not determined by the fact that our version contains the term; and that the term is non-null is therefore not version-dependent?"

24 Goodman, *Ways of Worldmaking*, p. 94.
25 Ibid., p. 103.

"That seems undeniable."

"Then our version did not after all make it happen that the Big Dipper in fact exists – that it is *there* to be denoted. Thus, our version did not, after all, make the Big Dipper."

8 CONCLUSION

Goodman concludes his paper by saying that "thinking should go straight when it can but sometimes has to find its way around corners."[26]

I should add that, in doing so, it needs to keep alert for hidden pitfalls around the bend. Can't we maneuver the corner safely by agreeing on pluralism and on version making, while avoiding the creation of parallel worlds?[27]

---

26 Goodman, "On Some Worldly Worries," p. 4.

27 In a work that appeared while this book was in press, Goodman has replied to this chapter in his "Comments," Chapter 15 of Peter McCormick, ed., "Star-making" (Boston: M.I.T. Press), 1996, pp. 203–13, esp. pp. 207–13. I regret to report that, despite several new points in his reply, our disagreement persists. I continue to maintain that a version of our making may purport to be true; whether it succeeds or not goes beyond the bare making, which therefore does not determine its truth, if true, nor create either the objects of which it speaks, or their alleged properties.

Index

acceptance, 168–9, 170
actors, 141
allusion, 148–9
Alston, William P., 74n
ambiguity, 7, 38, 198
  derivative compound, 41–4, 49
  derivative constituent, 39–42, 44
  E-ambiguity, 27–32, 51
  elementary, 27–32, 42–5, 51
  I-ambiguity, 32, 52, 54
  and indecision, 51–4
  in language, 25–49
  M-ambiguity, *see* meaning, multiple
  of occurrence, 32, 41
  pictorial, 7, 50–67
analyticity, 20–1
art, 97, 109, 110–26, 149
  allographic, 135, 152n, 159
  autographic, 134, 152n, 159
Austin, J. L., 139
authority, 121–6, 156–7

Beardsley, Monroe, 74n
Black, Max, 68n, 74n

caption, 11–12, 54–7, 63, 73
Cassirer, Ernst, 4, 9, 16, 130–2, 152–3
certainty, 163–5, 165–71, 173, 178–83
chain
  of exemplification, 148–9

of historic authorizations, 137, 152
characterization, 55–6
child, 47, 83–4, 100–9
Cohen, T., 75n
coherence, 168, 170–1, 175, 179–82
  see also consistency
community, 123–4, 129, 149, 158–60
completability, 60–1
compounds, 37, 40, 43–5, 49
  parallel, 34, 40, 46
confirmation statements, 172–9
consistency, 163–6, 169, 180, 182
Constable, John, 111–12
contextualism
  Goodman's, 74–80
  revised, 80–6
creation, 99–102
creativity, 108–9, 125
credibility, 180–2, 185–6

Dampier, William Cecil, 111
dance, 134
Davidson, Donald, 67n
Dember, W. N., 55n
demonstrative terms, 174, 177–8
denotation, 6, 11–21, 61, 116, 132–3,
  140, 144, 146, 148, 157, 196
Dewey, John, 3
discourse-dependence, 197–201
D–R, *see* duck–rabbit

Index